Art in the early years

For all involved in teaching young children, this timely book offers the necessary tools with which to develop a broad, creative and inspirational visual arts programme.

Presented in two parts, this text covers both theoretical and practical angles:

- Part I investigates contemporary early childhood art education, challenging what is traditionally considered an early years art experience
- Part II puts the theory to test by presenting the reader with numerous inventive visual art lessons that imaginatively meet goals for creative development issued by the QCA.

The author strikes the perfect balance between discussion of the subject and provision of hands-on material for use in lessons, which makes this book a complete art education resource for all involved in early years art education. Teachers, trainee teachers, or nursery teachers, who wish to implement a more holistic art curriculum in the classroom while meeting all the required standards, will find *Art in the early years* an essential companion.

Kristen Ali Eglinton is an art education consultant, practitioner and trainer and is owner of Canyon Arts based in England.

Teaching and learning in the early years
Series Editor *Joy Palmer*

This innovatory and up-to-date series is concerned specifically with curriculum practice in the first three years of school. Each book includes guidance on:

- subject content
- planning and organisation
- assessment and record-keeping
- in-service training

This practical advice is placed in the context of the National Curriculum and the latest theoretical work on how children learn at this age and what experiences they bring to their early years in the classroom.

Other books in the series:

Geography in the early years
Joy Palmer

History in the early years, second edition
Hilary Cooper

Mathematics in the early years
Wendy Clemson and David Clemson

Music in the early years
Aelwyn Pugh and Lesley Pugh

Physical education in the early years
Pauline Wetton

RE in the early years
Elizabeth Ashton

Special educational needs in the early years
Ruth A. Wilson

Art in the early years

Kristen Ali Eglinton

RoutledgeFalmer
Taylor & Francis Group

LONDON AND NEW YORK

First published 2003
by RoutledgeFalmer
11 New Fetter Lane, London EC4P 4EE

Simultaneously published in the USA and Canada
by RoutledgeFalmer
29 West 35th Street, New York, NY 10001

RoutledgeFalmer is an imprint of the Taylor & Francis Group

© 2003 Kristen Ali Eglinton

Typeset in Times New Roman by Keystroke, Jacaranda Lodge, Wolverhampton
Printed and bound in Great Britain by Biddles Ltd, Guildford and King's Lynn

British Library Cataloguing in Publication Data
A catalogue record for this book is available from the British Library

Library of Congress Cataloging in Publication Data
A catalog record for this book has been requested

ISBN 0–415–29846–6

Contents

Illustrations

FIGURES

TABLES

Acknowledgements

Scores of family, friends, and colleagues on both sides of the Atlantic have helped bring this book to fruition. Starting with the children and educators I have been privileged to work with, they are the inspiration for this book – to them I am greatly indebted. For help with the manuscript I sincerely wish to thank Diana MacLean for kind-heartedly reading the manuscript and contributing excellent suggestions. Early years trainer and practitioner Dawn Ridehalgh, who by lending materials, advice, and time, has supported this book since its conception. In addition, her reading of the manuscript supplied me with invaluable feedback. Eric and Nuala Roberts for suggesting necessary revisions to the manuscript, for giving advice that kept me calm and focused, and for much needed insight, and to Dr Mary Bachvarova, who, by taking the time to see the big picture, provoked and supported a wonderful transformation of the manuscript. Thanks to Alison Foyle at RoutledgeFalmer for believing 'art in the early years' is necessary, and for supporting it along the way. Love to the children (and especially their parents, aunts, and uncles!) who contributed their incredible artwork to this book including Bridget Hodgson, Madeleine Hodgson, Isabel Scoble, and baby Maxine Stillwagon. I must be wildly blessed because there really are too many people to mention who have lent support in other ways including heaps of friends across America and England – their phone calls and visits kept me in beautiful company. Gratitude to Chris and Reg Eglinton, my fabulous family right here in England. Jean and Stewart Pickering, creative pioneers, for giving me the opportunity to work with and learn from the talented educators and children at Kids Unlimited. My own teachers, especially Dr Joan Webster-Price artist and art education professor (CCNY) extraordinaire, a role model who has tremendously influenced my research and art. Special mention to Dr Crinson, School of Art History and Archaeology at the University of Manchester, for kindly and quickly helping me get what I needed to do my research.

Above all, it is to my family that I owe the most heartfelt gratitude. Foremost, to parents who make caring an art, Nancy and Fred Feingold. I could not have done this without them. Their tireless encouragement, support, and love have given me the confidence to realise even the most lofty imaginings – it is to them that I am most grateful. To Kimberly and Chris Palmer and Heather Weinstein for loudly rooting me on, for listening, and loving, and inspiring me with their dedication to humanity, to Ann Neill whose sunshine reaches me all the way in England, and in loving memory of Harold Neill, a true believer in learning. To Mark Eglinton, one of the most creative and resourceful people I have ever met, his visual and cerebral efforts are seen throughout this book. My biggest fan and most caring confidant, he ungrudgingly and unfailingly, gives me the time and support I need to create, teach, research, and write about art. It is to him that I dedicate this book.

Part I

Contemporary early childhood art education

Chapter 1

Setting the scene:

The why, what, and how of early years art education

INTRODUCTION

Art in the early years – the phrase evokes images of young children in colourful aprons up to their elbows in school paint, bright marks on paper clipped to a child-sized easel, little hands furiously pounding, squeezing, or moulding some malleable medium, the unmistakable feel of crayons or smell of play dough. Yet, though scores of us recollect these quintessential childhood art experiences, there is much more to the artistic education of young children than the splashing of paint, or the manipulation of art media. Some of the art lessons children partake in, while devised by educators with the best intentions, often fall short of delivering any educational or developmental benefits. As Part I of this text demonstrates, art in early childhood is often characterised by activities that offer little more than a chance to, perhaps, get messy, or play with art media. What is more, the common non-interventionist approach of merely sitting a child in front of a lump of clay, although seemingly educationally sound, can ultimately lead to boredom and dissatisfaction. Partly because of this widespread practice and narrow view of what art in early childhood could potentially offer, many educators fail to understand the importance of art in the early years, and possess, at best, only a vague notion of how to support the artistic learning of young children.

This book extends the limited definition of what is traditionally considered an artistic experience – art production or the making of form – and takes a more expansive and holistic approach further incorporating aesthetic experiences (experiences with beauty), and encounters with art (reflecting on and growing from works of art, craft, and the like). In a holistic art programme, the three types of art experiences form a highly related structure, in which all of the elements in the model influence each of the other elements. Art making might include a previous encounter with art or sometimes an aesthetic experience will spark an idea for art making. Art making, encounters with art, and aesthetic experiences work together, their union forms a comprehensive art programme. This relationship is demonstrated in Figure 1.1.

In the model presented, all artistic experiences are dynamic; experience leads to more experiences; discovery generates further investigation. However, art

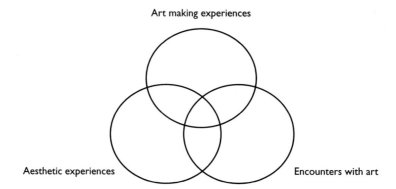

Figure 1.1 Artistic experiences and a comprehensive art programme include art making experiences as well as aesthetic experiences and encounters with art. In a holistic programme, all three components are integrated

experiences are only dynamic if educators play an active role. The educator propels the experience by engaging children in dialogue, stimulating them through motivation, observing children when they make art, talk, and play, employing documentation, and reflecting on art products. In this approach, art experiences work like a web, each discovery, interest, and dialogue is connected, taking children to new meaningful artistic endeavours.

Part I of this book is devoted to addressing art's essential role in the early years, and to offering educators the theoretical, historical, and ideological base from which they can create their own educational early years art programme. Included is an exploration of erroneous teaching practices, an in-depth study of artistic experiences, the 'process', art making experiences, and motivation and dialogue (Chapter 2), aesthetic experiences and encounters with art (Chapter 3), the role of documentation (Chapter 4); and art for special needs (Chapter 4). Finally, Chapter 5 thoroughly examines the early learning goals for creative development issued by the Qualifications and Curriculum Authority (QCA) (2000), and looks at implementation of those goals into effective art in the early years practice. Part II of this text offers readers a multitude of sound educational artistic experiences.

A few explanations, clarifications, and comments before beginning; first, this book continuously refers to children in the 'foundation stage': children aged 3 to 5 or to the end of reception year. This does not mean, however, that with slight modifications the basic principles and practices explored in Part I and the experiences in Part II are not applicable in some form to a wide range of ages. Further, even within the Foundation Stage, the varying ages and levels of development will require educators to adjust the offered methods and experiences. Second, the terms educator, staff, and teacher are used interchangeably, they include, but are not limited to, anyone involved or interested in the arts education of young children: teachers, nursery nurses, teacher trainers, nursery staff and

managers, students of childcare and early years study, parents, school admin-
istrators, art education students, and the like. Third, settings in this book are referred
to as classrooms, nurseries, or early years environments, to name a few. This
expansive view enables educators to envision an art programme in their own
particular teaching situation. Finally, though it is not required, a thoughtful read
of Part I is highly recommended before embarking upon the experiences presented
in Part II.

WHY ART?

Whereas the educational importance of a maths or reading programme is
rarely questioned, one can safely assume when promoting and implementing a
comprehensive visual arts agenda, educators will find much of their precious
time used justifying the need for art in education. Experience reveals handfuls
of meetings spent tirelessly defending the positive consequences of an extensive
arts curriculum. Some educators are fortunate, on their side are like-minded people
who support the idea of art in education; yet, we frequently find that many of these
like-minded supporters have a limited understanding as to why art is so essential
to a child's education. They recognise that experiences with art should be available
to children, but remain unaware of the vast opportunity for development embedded
in art experiences. In order to create an art programme or even one simple art
experience, it is imperative that we understand both the character of art and the
developmental opportunities housed in artistic experiences – it is only when we
know why we teach art that we can teach it in a truly worthwhile way.

There are many reasons why educators supply children with art media or supplies.
Objectives range from sensory exploration to the exercising of the imagination.
Observation and experience demonstrate that in the pre-school and nursery, sensory
stimulation, as an artistic objective, is at the top of the list. This is a wonderful aim.
Art experiences do stimulate the senses; however, the idea is to go deeper, to expose
the depth and breadth of potential goodness tucked away inside artistic experiences.
    Eisner (1972: 2) describes two educational rationales for engaging in art
experiences: the 'contextualist' and 'essentialist'. The contextualist looks first
at the context in which the art programme will unfold, and, after considering the
surrounding circumstances, creates art experiences to fill the recognised need.
The objectives of the art programme are fashioned on 'who the child is, what
type of needs the community has, what problems the larger society is facing'
(ibid.: 3). The contextualist will teach art, for example, to build self-esteem,
unleash creativity, or as a tool in the enrichment of another subject such as science
or maths.
    The essentialist, on the other hand, creates an art programme based on the
nature of art itself; the essentialist 'emphasizes what is indigenous and unique to
art' (ibid.: 2), and believes 'that the most important contributions of art are those

that only art can provide' (ibid.: 7). The essentialist examines the distinguishing features of art and bases the art programme on those characteristics. Sharpening the senses, heightening perception, the giving of form to ideas and thoughts, and the fostering of aesthetic awareness are some examples of what only art can contribute.

An examination of the contextualist objectives and the essentialist rationale is a good starting point for studying the reasons why we teach art. Looking closely at the contextualist aims, one is reminded of pre-school and nursery settings, community art projects, and numerous non-learning establishments such as crèches or after-school clubs. Art projects are justified as facilitators of physical development, as a way to build the self-esteem of the children, or as a project for the betterment of the community, fulfilled, for example, by the fabrication of a community mural where young and old have an opportunity to work together. There should be no mistake, these are excellent reasons for promoting the arts; not only are they valid, they also expose children to some of the many benefits of art. However, there is much more to art than merely the opportunity to, say, hone fine motor skills or build community spirit. The following section describes some of the major reasons for teaching art. A number of the justifications are quite detailed, others only touched upon; the reasons for teaching art are so numerous and diverse it is impossible to explain each one in detail in this particular text. See Table 1.1 for an overview of the justifications.

The senses

Both the contextualist and the essentialist agree that the senses and the subsequent stimulation of them are a just rationale for the teaching of art. The senses do more than feel, see, hear, smell, and taste; the senses connect us with the

Table 1.1 Overview, reasons for teaching art in the early years

Reason
Cultivate sensory awareness, education of the senses
Growth of perceptual discernment, the engagement in active perception
Development of aesthetic awareness, developing sensitivity to the natural and constructed environment
Cognitive development, developing an understanding of the world, how to construct meaning, and engaging in symbolic activity
Communication of a visual language
Exercising intuitive thinking
Perpetuation of cultural and artistic knowledge and practices
Language, social, personal, physical, imaginative, and creative development

environment. From birth, a person explores the environment through the senses; the senses are in essence the channels through which we extract information from the environment and, consequently, learn. Lowenfeld and Brittain (1987: 11) state, 'It is only through the senses that learning can take place.' Moreover, most inspiration, stimulation, and information come from sources outside us. One can argue that, perhaps, all internal experiences, including the formulation of original ideas, are sparked by external stimuli. Yet, as Eisner (1985) points out, in education the nurturing of the senses is overlooked in the quest for the advancement of the mind. How the senses came to be divorced from learning is a matter best left to the educational historian. For our purposes, suffice to say that art experiences reconnect the senses with learning. How? Art experiences, when properly facilitated, serve to sharpen and cultivate sensory awareness. Sensitivity to our environment does not just happen, Lowenfeld and Brittain (1987) explain that the senses need to be properly educated to see subtly and distinction, to feel gradations, to become truly aware of our surroundings. Rich and worthwhile art experiences awaken and ultimately guide the senses.

Perceptual development

Keiler (1977: 19) describes perception as 'the significant impression which an object or an event produces on the mind through the various senses'. Keiler (ibid.: 19) adds, we 'exercise discrimination' in perception. He explains that this distinction is caused by our being 'impressed by *one* particular aspect of perceived reality than by any other'. It is based on this phenomenon that Keiler attributes the difference between looking and seeing. How does all this theory answer the question, why art? What does perception and perceptual discrimination have to do with art in early childhood? The answer comes in two parts.

First, art provides the material that enables the growth of a child's perceptual discernment. Looking at, reflecting upon, creating, and experiencing art teaches, guides and refines perception. Second, perception is not limited to impressions through the senses; true perception requires thought. Taking this notion a step further, Arnheim (1969) demonstrates in his book *Visual Thinking*, the inextricable link between thought and perception; he reveals that thinking is fed by perception and perception by thought. Since a large portion of perception is visual, this uncovered relationship has huge implications for the arts, namely the visual arts (Arnheim 1983). If thinking and perception are tied, it follows then that the active perception, which is part of art experiences, is more than just looking – it is thinking, learning, and as Arnheim (1983) concludes, understanding vital visual and conceptual relationships. The visual arts provide a place for the child to look, think, understand, and learn.

Aesthetic awareness

Educators and authors involved in early childhood art often point out the difference between using the word aesthetic as a noun and employing it as an adjective (Hagaman 1990; Herberholz and Hanson 1995). The word aesthetic as a noun refers to a branch of philosophy that examines the nature of art and artworks, as an adjective, the word simply means relating to and/or an appreciation of beauty. In Chapter 3 we look closer at aesthetics and its involvement in early childhood art; for now, it is sufficient to say, in the early years we are concerned with the word aesthetic as an adjective – again, relating to and/or an appreciation of beauty.

When we use the word as an adjective, it becomes easy to appreciate the notion that art education aids in the growth of aesthetic awareness. When children are taught how to sense and perceive with refinement and skill, they are more apt to recognise or discover beauty or, we will call it, the *aesthetic* in objects and experiences that before held little interest as an actual aesthetic object or experience. Lowenfeld and Brittain (1987: 129) describe aesthetics as 'a basic way of relating oneself to the environment'. They believe that forming a sensitivity to the environment, including how we perceive it visually, feel it, and live in it is in fact the development of aesthetic awareness.

Art opens children up to the infinite aesthetic objects and experiences that present themselves everyday. If we fail to support the recognition of beauty, a child's world can soon become barren and undistinguished, inspiration and stimulation over time are replaced with passivity and disregard for both the natural and shaped environment.

Cognitive development

Cognitive development is described by Papalia and Olds (1993: 29) as the 'changes in children's thought processes that result in a growing ability to acquire and use knowledge about their world'. Cognitive development applies to art in two respects. First, the child is constantly interacting with the environment, learning how to look, feel, and ultimately express. It is in this continuous interaction that the child will form a deeper understanding of the world, better methods for extracting vital information, and formulate new and original ways to give visual form to their experiences, thoughts, and ideas. Second, as Gardner (1990: 9) reasons, looking at, and creating art require a child to arrive at the encounter equipped with basic methods for both 'decoding' and creating symbols. This symbolic activity rooted in art created and reflected upon is indicative of arts cognitive contribution.

The remaining justifications for the teaching of art, while just as important as those previously described, are mentioned here briefly. Furthermore, though numerous school subjects can target some of these remaining areas, art continues to be an excellent vehicle for their facilitation. They include, communication in a visual language, the use of intuitive thinking, and the perpetuation of culture and art's rich history (see Chapter 3 for an in-depth look at art history and the transmission of culture), language development, personal and social development, and creative growth.

Our understanding of the educational benefits of art experiences and the deeper awareness of why we teach art provide us with the foundation on which to construct artistic experiences. However, before beginning this construction, we look at why we must often rally support for an art programme that stretches beyond the traditional concept of childhood art.

WHAT HAPPENED TO ART EDUCATION?

Baker (1992) found that although 50 per cent of nursery time in the ten schools studied was spent in an artistic activity, most of the activities lacked value, quality, and fell significantly short of exposing children to art's educational benefits. Additionally, observation and experience indicate most educators recognise they should be having art experiences with children, but do not have a real understanding of how to teach art. If, as we just learned, art is indispensable to a child's education, why do educators have such a limited understanding? How did art become a peripheral subject, something not seen as academic or as vital to the curriculum?

There are countless reasons why the visual arts in early childhood education is rarely utilised as a discipline full of possibility and worthy of serious study. Some of these reasons include the perpetuation of erroneous and outdated teaching methods, the lack of goals, and the tendency to use art as a tool in the teaching of another seemingly more 'important' subject. However, simply offering a list does not support a real appreciation of the causes. To understand why art in the early years has never reached its full educational potential, a brief look at the history and theories of art education is necessary. It is in the history and theoretical base of art education that modern practices in early childhood art originate.

Art education's history and theory: a brief study

Art education has its roots in various areas of study, including general education, psychology, and the discipline of art itself. Additionally, because we are looking at art in the early years, we can include contributions from the field of early childhood education. Throughout history, at any one time, there might be several disciplines involved in and guiding the course art education.

Before the twentieth century, child art was considered an undeveloped and unsophisticated version of adult art. Leeds (1989) points out, this view soon took a drastic turn, and by the close of the first quarter of the twentieth century, many people, including celebrated modern artists, regarded children's art as possessing its very own aesthetic value. Leeds maintains this change of opinion was produced by the attention of modern artists and a new interest in childhood as an area of study.

Various educators, artists, and theorists active during the first part of the century were responsible for altering prevailing attitudes towards children's art, and for shaping present art education methodology. At the turn of the century, psychologist G. Stanley Hall believed it was the teacher's job to study the child rather than the academic subject; that education should follow from the needs of the child. Continuing from Hall, and committed to the study of children and education, was the theorist and philosopher, John Dewey. Dewey proposed that knowledge was gained through interaction with the environment, and that in order for these occurrences to be meaningful, the individual child's experience must be taken into account. Dewey also believed that learning should lead to more learning, that we are active learners, and that 'schools needed to provide physical, emotional, and intellectual freedom for the pupil' (Eisner and Ecker 1966: 8). In 1920, Dewey's philosophy led to the establishment of the Progressive Education Association in the United States and, consequently, to the opening of 'progressive schools'. The progressive schools stressed the freedom to explore, invent, and express oneself; art's position was at the centre of the curriculum. Yet, as Eisner and Ecker (1966: 9) point out, though it was not Dewey's intention, his proponents, the leaders of the Progressive Education Association, soon interpreted and advanced his ideas 'into a movement which eventually considered self-expression and non-interference by the teacher an important tenet of its program'. The progressives 'were committed to the idea that art ability unfolded, as a flower did, when the proper environment was provided' (Eisner 1972: 52). Further solidifying the call for non-intervention was the emerging view that children naturally progress through stages of artistic growth, and these stages happen spontaneously – in other words, it was now assumed children could develop in art without our help (ibid).

Similar in ideology to Dewey and Hall, working at the turn of the century, was Viennese artist and educator Franz Cizek. Cizek believed the child should have the freedom to create without any interference from the outside world. He thought that children were already in possession of all they needed to create and express themselves. Cizek opened an art school for children in Vienna in 1897. The school was soon famous as a place where children could go and create with freedom. As Leeds (1989: 99) writes, 'The school became an important model for progressive art education movements throughout the world.'

The view held by the progressives, that outside intervention could perhaps damage artistic maturation or taint the child's creative nature, and the suggestion that a child's artistic development unfolds naturally without the support of outside sources permeated the first half of the twentieth century, and was perpetuated throughout Europe and the United States in the second half. The non-interventionist approach to art teaching – still the accepted norm in most modern nursery and pre-schools throughout the world – is a direct consequence of this outdated ideology (Eisner 1972; Kindler 1996) (see Chapter 2 for more information on the non-interventionist approach). Unlike most other subjects, where we believe we must guide children providing information and skills to ensure successful learning experiences, in art the consensus has been to allow for what is described as a natural 'unfolding' (Gardner 1976: 99).

Beginning in the latter part of the first half of the century and continuing through the second half, the emphasis in art education shifted to the study of both creativity, specifically art's role in cultivating it, and child behaviour (Eisner 1972). Many psychologists, child-behaviour experts, and major influential art educators sought to employ art, not as a discipline, but as a means of nurturing and tapping into a child's creativity. Others began to view art as a subject that, because of its sensuous properties and visible outpourings, allowed for a child's emotional release and offered adults a way to read or analyse a child's deepest feelings. Together with other aforementioned ideologies and occurrences, the labelling of art as a catalyst in the growth of creativity, and as an instrument in the release of emotional, physical, and psychological energy, resulted in art losing its discipline base, and becoming exploited for various educational and developmental ends (Eisner and Ecker 1966). The exploitation of art continues straight into today's classroom practices. Teaching art to enhance another evidently more important subject, allowing children to interact with art media for the sole purpose of 'getting their frustrations out', or regarding art as a sacred activity, something not to be taught, but something that will magically unfold are practices that, though their seeds were planted over a century ago, still flower today.

The introduction of *discipline-based art education* (DBAE) in the early 1980s saw a shift in the objectives of art educators. DBAE recognises the essentialist justifications for the teaching of art, and highlights art as possessing a body of knowledge that includes the disciplines of art history, art criticism, art production, and aesthetics. Supporters of DBAE believe art is a vital part of every child's education. By making art a subject of study, proponents of DBAE hope to 'educationalise' art again (Getty 1985). Indeed, at present there are many approaches and models, for example, Project Zero's Arts PROPEL (see Gardner 1989), that strive to create a more inclusive and holistic (interrelated) art education practice, offering time for reflection, experiences with art history, as well as art production. Nevertheless, though the focus on art as a subject of study has gathered momentum in formal schooling, it has not quite taken hold in early childhood education. Even though educators are learning through experience and observation that sensitive intervention is vital to artistic growth, early childhood art education is still clinging to the ineffective non-intervention or so-called *laissez-faire* approach to teaching art (Brittain 1979; Edwards and Nabors 1993; Eglinton 2002; Kindler 1995, 1996).

After looking at the history of art education, it would be incorrect to blame today's educator. Training programmes in early childhood education rarely offer the in-depth guidance staff need to develop valuable art experiences (Kindler

1996). Generally, teachers will teach what they know, and it is obvious from art education's imperfect past that most teachers, during their own education, rarely participated in appropriate art experiences (ibid.). These same educators come into classrooms carrying long-held beliefs about what art is, and what art in education means. The majority of teachers have the best intentions, they make sure art materials are available for sensory exploration, but many have little understanding that the child's sensory investigation will soon give way to a need to give form to feelings, thoughts, and ideas. Staff allow time to create art, but because they lack the confidence and skills necessary for teaching art, do not use that time to unmask art's massive possibilities for cognitive, aesthetic, and perceptual growth. As a result, the notion that art does not need to be taught, that art learning will unfold, or that art plays only a marginal role in a child's education is, inevitably, sustained (Kindler 1996; Szyba 1999). Faced with these misconceptions, ingrained attitudes and beliefs, and inadequate skills, the educator rallying support for a holistic art programme is faced with an arduous task.

On a final note, until recently any specified objectives for artistic development in the early years were vague and difficult to ascertain. Couple the limited training with the fact that early years educators had no established goals, and it should not surprise us that the art education of children has suffered tremendously. The new early learning goals issued by the Qualification and Curriculum Authority (QCA 2000) give us, at the very least, a starting point for devising an inclusive and developmentally appropriate art programme.

Recognising art's indispensable role in overall development, and examining the pattern of events that has led to early years art practices, form an excellent starting point for creating an exciting art programme. We now need to know the baseline from which we can thoughtfully guide artistic learning, facilitate art experiences, and, when fitting, intervene in children's artistic endeavours. In short, a general understanding of artistic maturation is fundamental. Accordingly, the next section looks at the early stages of artistic development.

ARTISTIC DEVELOPMENT

Theories about the artistic development of children vary. While some theorists support an organic linear unfolding that remains unaffected by outside influences, others believe emotional, social, and other factors have an effect on artistic growth (Kindler 1996). Promoting a linear unfolding, Lowenfeld and Brittain (1987: 37) state, 'Children draw in predictable ways, going through fairly definite stages, starting with the first marks on paper and progressing through adolescence.' On the other hand, Gardner (1980) believes artistic expression follows a *U-shaped* model where expression in art peaks in early childhood, dips when a child enters formal schooling around age six, and rises again in adolescence. Gardner (ibid.: 12) considers artistic development dynamic and writes that many models leave us 'with a sterile, static view of the child drawer'.

Aside from the debate between proponents supporting a natural unfolding of artistic development and those promoting a more non-linear model, educators and theorists have long been reflecting upon and documenting a so-called 'normal' model of artistic development that presents itself in a typical, supportive environment. Because we are searching for a simple developmental model from which we can understand children's talents and create for them developmentally suitable art experiences, we focus on points of commonality found in the texts of these educators and strengthened by our own personal observation (Chapman 1978; Brittain 1979; Gardner 1980; Herberholz and Hanson 1995; Kellogg 1969; Lowenfeld and Brittain 1987).

A few points should be noted. First, although maturation is presented in stages, art knowledge, cultural and aesthetic awareness, and the like must be carefully fostered in order to take root and thrive. The environment, the experiences children have, and the educator, among other variables, all play a part in a child's artistic development. Second, the basis for our developmental model is 'optimistic'; the stages are only the starting point. In fact, it is with apprehension that the stages of development are offered, it is so easy to see them as the apex, rather than what they are – the developmental baseline. Third, although age ranges are specified, they are only a guide. Finally, as our focus is the Foundation Stage, maturation is described from birth to age 7 only. For easy reference, Table 1.2 provides a general overview of the developmental stages (birth to age seven).

Table 1.2 Stages of artistic development – birth to age seven

Pre-scribbling stage	Scribbling stage	Schema stage
Babies react to the environment.	Age begins: between one to two years of age.	Age begins: anywhere from three and a half years to five and a half years lasts until approximately age seven.
Full sensory interaction.	Divided into three parts: Random scribbling –	
Learn they can make an 'impression' on the environment.	children's first marks.	Early schema stage marked by early symbol use (for example, the 'head-feet' representation).
Show visual preference.	Controlled scribbling – children have better control over media, marks more intentional. Children generally move into controlled scribbling six months after beginning random scribbling.	Drawing employed to represent, describe, and give form to feelings.
		As the stage progresses schemas become more complex and varied.
	Named scribbling – marks now seen as representative, children name their scribbles.	

Stages of artistic development

Early activity reveals the human desire to act on and respond to the environment using the body as a vehicle for that interaction. Children smear their food across their plate, are calmed by the soft feel of their favourite blanket, or are excited by the splash produced when they strike a hand into a puddle or tub of water. These first interactions signify a need for people to express themselves and connect with the world through sensory means; the earliest of those means is kinaesthetic (relating to motion). By the end of the first year of life, children are aware they can deliberately make a mark or imprint upon the environment; in addition, from birth, children show 'visual preferences', in other words, they will look at some stimulus for a longer period of time than others (Papalia and Olds 1993: 159).

Approximately, between the ages of one and two children will make their first mark with typical art media. This period of the *scribbling stage* is referred to as *random scribbling* (see Figure 1.2). These first marks, usually reflective of the child's movement, are often thought motivated by kinaesthetic reward; however, Kellogg (1969: 7) argues that visual involvement plays as big a part in scribbling as the satisfaction derived from movement. 'Why', she asks, 'is a steamy window attractive only as long as the steam lasts to show the lines the child's finger traces?' These first marks, Kellogg points out, are meaningful rather than meaningless, and our attention and encouragement throughout this stage are vital if our desire is for children to reach their full artistic potential.

On average, six months after beginning to scribble, children move into a phase called *controlled scribbling* (Figure 1.3). This transition, often passing unnoticed by adults, is an important turning point. It is during this time in the scribbling stage that children realise they are able to control media and subsequent mark making. They begin to hold and manipulate drawing media with greater adeptness than previously exhibited. Children are more aware of the paper's boundaries and drawing becomes intentional (though not fully).

Figure 1.2 Random scribbling. Maxine age 1.3 years makes some of her first marks

Figure 1.3 Controlled scribbling. Isabel age 1.11 years makes more intentional marks

   Soon after controlled scribbling, children begin to name their scribbles; this developmental milestone referred to as *named scribbling*, marks a huge cognitive-perceptual event. Children now see their marks as representative of something other than kinaesthetic record; the result is 'a change from kinaesthetic thinking to imaginative thinking' (Lowenfeld and Brittain 1987: 193). How does this happen? The most widely held belief, as illustrated by Lowenfeld and Brittain (1987), is that children begin to see and recall forms in their scribbles. What were once just lines of motion now become lines around forms; the areas inside the lines take on special significance. An excellent example of named scribbling is seen in Figure 1.4. As the child scribbled, the outline of a heart emerged; the child noticed the heart as quickly as the ink flowed from her pen and exclaimed with delight 'heart!'

   During this period, children start to talk more about what they are drawing, often narrating as they move the crayon across the paper. Children might begin some drawings with an intention of what they want to draw, they may create purely for sensory exploration or, what often happens is, drawings started with an idea soon become sensory explorations and sensory explorations soon turn into named drawings. Some lines will become shapes that represent objects, other lines, or, sometimes even the media itself will represent a feeling, idea, expression, or motion; for example, it is not uncommon to observe a child quickly moving a pencil across paper while proclaiming some imaginary thought such as 'the car went so fast!' (Brittain 1979). In any of the scenarios, the child cannot predict the finished product for it is constantly changing and developing throughout the drawing process (ibid.).

   Evolving out of the scribbling stage, beginning anywhere from three and a half years to five and a half years and lasting until approximately age seven, is the *schema stage*. Schema refers to simple forms or symbols used to represent objects. Indicative to the nature of development, emergence into this stage is gradual; Figure 1.5 is a brilliant example of the foggy line between stages of

Named Heart

Figure 1.4 Named scribbling by Bridget age 2.7 years

Figure 1.5 Example of blurry line between stages of development. Bridget age 3.1 years
is moving into the schematic stage

Figure 1.6 'Head–feet' representation in schematic stage by Madeleine age 4.2 years

development. The young child who did this drawing is slowly moving into the schema stage, but still part of the named scribbling period. To illustrate, though the markings on the page indicate an exploration of shapes, often seen in the named scribbling phase, the symbol or schema used to represent the named 'monster' is characteristic of the early schematic stage. Some texts break up the schema stage into two distinct parts: the *pre-schematic stage* and *schematic stage*; however, as observed in Figure 1.5, the boundaries between the stages are quite hazy, consequently, in this book, both stages are referred to as the schema stage. Moving into this period and using symbols, however simple, is a major developmental step. Typical of this stage is the 'head–feet' representation of a human (Figure 1.6). The explanations as to why children depict a human in this fashion are numerous; readers may want to refer to Gardner (1980) or Kellogg (1969) for an in-depth exploration of the subject.

In the schema stage, drawing is used to represent, describe, or turn feelings or experiences into form. Adults can now easily use the work of children as the basis for discussion and further artistic growth. As children continue to develop, they will modify and add to their original symbols. By the age of six or seven, children's drawings are quite complex, varied, and symbolically advanced.

What can children do in art? And when can they do it? It is fruitless to compose a list of skills children are able to accomplish at selected ages. Skills, such as knowing the right amount of glue to use or how to properly work scissors, are effortlessly acquired within the context of art experiences when a child appears developmentally ready to learn them. In addition, and perhaps most importantly, a child's promise in art is not based on how perfectly they can, say, render a flower or demonstrate with virtuosity easily learned skills, but rather, more aptly, on aesthetic and perceptual growth, cultural awareness, innovation, and use of the imagination, to name a few. What young children are capable of, regardless of their stage of artistic development, lies beyond our traditional notion of art activities;

and finds its place among those artistic experiences we have not yet discovered, or may have cast aside as too complex or sophisticated. Bruner (1961: 47) believes, and quite rightly so, that by adapting material and paying attention to the developmental framework 'there is no reason to believe that any subject cannot be taught to any child at virtually any age in some form'.

Chapter 2

A work in progress:

The process, art experiences, and art making

This chapter examines the creating of art experiences, specifically a type of art experience called art making. However, before beginning, it is necessary to lay the groundwork exploring the idea of the process, exposing some inefficient teaching practices, and looking at the role of the adult in children's artistic development.

THEY SAY 'IT IS PROCESS THAT COUNTS', BUT WHAT DOES THAT REALLY MEAN?

When thinking about constructing an art programme or, for that matter, one simple art experience in the early years, many educators automatically articulate a required focus on the process. Indeed, most of us involved in early childhood education have probably heard the comment 'in art, it is the process and not the product that is important'; in fact, it has become something of a motto, but do we really know what it means? At first, it appears to be an uncomplicated statement, which, upon initial reflection, we presume refers to one of two things. One, we focus on the process in an effort to avoid dwelling upon the finished product. The belief is that by looking at and discussing the product, we automatically make judgements, and art critiques, of any kind, do not belong in the early childhood classroom. The second presumption is that a focus on the process refers to the benefits of sensory exploration that is an inherent part of using art media. They imagine children 'in the process', delighted, laughing, swept away, feeling, smelling, and seeing colour and texture. They view early childhood art as a sensory extravaganza; they believe sensory discovery is all that matters, the product does not even enter the equation.

Are our presumptions correct? Do we accurately understand why the process is so important? Yes and no. The saying 'it's the process and not the product', or any variant on that theme, in reality, means many things. Foremost, yes; the process, or the steps children go through to make art, is undoubtedly more important than whether or not the finished product exemplifies the skilled work of a great master. However, as we soon learn, this does not mean the product should be overlooked or totally disregarded; the product, we discover, is a major part of the process itself. Regarding the second notion that a focus on the process refers to sensory stimulation, again yes; the sensory exploration that is traditionally part of art making is full of educational possibilities and should certainly be emphasised. In Chapter 1, we discovered the nurturing of the senses is an important educational aim; it is through the senses that we extract information from the environment and learn. However, we shortly find the active use of the senses may be *part* of a process, but it is not the whole process; there is much more to the process than the stimulation of the senses.

It is apparent that we need to probe deeper to comprehend this suddenly elusive phrase. A good working definition of the process would be:

A method or procedure one uses to bring about change or a particular end. Each step in the process leads to a transformation; this transformation during the process is reciprocal, participants affect or cause a transformation to the process, and the process, in some way, affects or transforms the participants.

If someone is 'in the process', they are in the middle of this transformation, they are involved in both creating and carrying out the transformation and, at the same time, their absorption in the process has an effect or transforms them. How does this definition apply to art experiences?

In art experiences, the child goes through a process or a *series of steps*. This process has an effect on the child: during the course of the procedure the child learns or discovers something, as a result the child's knowledge is altered. Because the child's knowledge is affected or transformed, the child simultaneously changes the experience: the newly acquired knowledge prompts the application of this knowledge in the form of either a new or an extended experience. For example, imagine during the process or 'procedure' of an art making experience a child discovers that using a larger paintbrush makes thicker paint marks on the paper. This new discovery, depending on an educator's involvement and the child's desire to further explore this finding, changes the path of the experience and, at the same time, alters the participant's view or concept of, in our example, how different sizes/types of paintbrushes make different marks. Also, consider that it is usually during the process of art experience itself that the tangible outpouring leads to a furtherance of expression. A five-year study by Brittain (1979: 12) found that when children made art, 'certain parts of the picture reminded a child of other things, so that the meaning of the drawing as it developed would change, and the completed parts would be incorporated into a new theme'. This is the process in action, the reciprocal effect between the process and the participant.

Why is a focus on the process so important? The process functions as a vehicle delivering art's educational attributes. The process is necessary to acquire new knowledge, learning, and developing. In Chapter 1 we learned about the developmental benefits of artistic experiences. Here we learn that these rewards including cognitive, aesthetic, and perceptual development are realised *within the process*, during art experiences. It is important to note, these are different types of experiences, because they use or require different processes or procedures, and offer individuals different educational gains. For instance, the process involved in drawing a picture is quite different from the procedure or process one would use to create a pot on the pottery wheel. In this comparison, the process used in drawing promotes, at the very least, a change in a child's cognitive development, by prompting the assimilation of information from the environment, and the creation of symbolic form. On the other hand, the process used in making pottery supports a change in the child's sensory development by affecting and influencing spacial and kinaesthetic awareness. Processes used in other art experiences might support the construction of new concepts, skill acquisition, or aesthetic development. It is, therefore, in order to acquire new knowledge, learn, and develop that we must support and focus on the process.

It needs to be understood that our overarching definition of artistic experiences, which includes art making, encounters with art, and aesthetic experiences requires us to recognise that process is not exclusive to art making. Both aesthetic experiences and encounters with art each independently possess their own process and, at the same time, are part of the *overall* process involved in artistic experience. To illustrate, discoveries made during the process of an aesthetic experience might lead to an art making experience, or while moving through the process in an art making experience, an investigation may lead to an encounter with art. It is important at this point to emphasise two key points:

1   On a grand scale, artistic experience is a process, each discovery changing the child and pointing to a new experience, each experience leading us into new investigations; it is a never-ending cycle.
2   In art making experiences, the lofty position of the process by no means negates the product. The product is the touchable offshoot of an art making process. Katz (1998: 34) writes of the celebrated Reggio Emilia municipal schools in northern Italy, 'graphic representations serve as resources for further exploration and deepening knowledge of the topic'. In art making experiences, the process encompasses the resulting product, and generates a change in those reflecting upon that product; furthermore, this reflection often leads to subsequent artistic experiences.

The misguided notion of what the process really is, and the consequent promotion of it either as a way to avoid the possible judging of the product or as a time for unguided sensory exploration, have served to perpetuate ineffective art in the early years. Accordingly, before exploring appropriate methodology, in an effort to stop the propagation of unsound approaches, we review a few of these various flawed practices, discover why they are invalid, and in our exploration begin to identify our role as educators in children's artistic experiences.

FAMILIAR APPROACHES TO EARLY CHILDHOOD ART

Many educators, convinced that a focus on the process simply means the occupying of the senses in the manipulation of art media, do not see themselves as part of children's art endeavours. Trying to maintain distance so as not to disturb the children's 'artistic flow', educators offer materials, but refrain from getting involved. Proving our point, Kindler (1996) argues that highlighting the process has led to the widespread promotion of a non-interventionist approach (see Chapter 1 for the roots of the non-interventionist approach). The non-interventionist method is clear-cut. Educators give children art media and allow time to make art, but they themselves do not take part in the child's experience. There is no meaningful dialogue or motivation. Art experiences are limited to sensory exercises that do not move the child through any kind of educational process – children simply proceed through the experience without any notable effects to their development. In the non-interventionist method, even if there are small discoveries or acquisitions of new knowledge along the way, without the teacher supporting children by, for example, highlighting the ways to use a new finding, children's sensory explorations inevitably lead to nowhere. If it is during the process that art's educational benefits are realised and absorbed, and exercises typical of the non-interventionist approach do not follow any teacher-supported process, it must be that much art making in the non-interventionist classroom is devoid of positive developmental attributes.

Expanding upon this idea, it is fitting to point out a familiar non-interventionist variety of teaching, what D'Amico and Buchman (1972: 4) call the 'materials approach'. Though the materials approach initially acquired its name because of the popular usage of various found and recycled media in collage or construction, the principle behind the approach applies to all art media. In practice, the method is just as it sounds, educators leave out, or make available in some way, art media and hope the child will be intrinsically motivated to create. Although an exploration of media is initially acceptable, for the same reasons as the non-interventionist approach, the materials approach does not have any educational benefits. There is minimal process involved, and without teacher involvement, even the smallest discoveries cannot be capitalised on. Further, this method breeds frustration, when children long to know how to employ media in the giving of form to their expression, or boredom, when they cannot think of any more ways to use a particular art medium nor see a medium's potential.

Another widespread practice in early years art, different to the non-intervention approach, but nonetheless wildly popular, is called the teacher-directed or 'product-oriented' activity (Edwards and Nabors 1993: 77). We have all seen the teacher-directed activity; the finished product already envisioned (one has probably already been fabricated), most of the materials are pre-cut or formed, and there are a series of steps the child will need to follow in order to create a product that closely resembles the adult model. For example, an activity that calls for a child to create, say, a paper cut-out teddy by taking pre-cut shapes and gluing them to the correct place on the 'teddy template'. There are many reasons why teachers feel compelled to offer these activities. Rationales include, wanting the parents to recognise the children's art, limited exposure to proper artistic experiences, lack of teacher confidence, or the need to bring structure to the classroom (Szyba 1999). Unfortunately, for both children and educators, teacher-directed projects do not possess a meaningful process. Yes, there are steps children go through to complete the product, but the steps taken do not have an effect on the child or the given experience. The activity is mapped out, the child cannot change or affect the course of the process, and the fixed steps rarely allow for discovery. Further, because the experience is predetermined even if a discovery does take place, there is no breadth offered for the child to explore or apply the new finding. Neither teachers nor children gain anything from these experiences; moreover, Szyba explains that teacher-directed art projects can have a negative effect on the child, possibly harming artistic confidence and development.

Yet despite the negative consequences or ineffectiveness of these approaches, some teachers may argue that there is, in fact, an educational process; that the child is learning valuable skills, such as how to tear paper or hold a crayon. Although, as the following illustrates, none of the named approaches are the proper vehicle for the acquisition of skills, this common rationale deserves a moment of attention.

In the non-intervention and materials approach, the rationale is that children are exposed to media that they in turn can experiment with, manipulate, and subsequently learn how to use. However, this argument fails to recognise that art media alone does not possess the power to teach skills, and we know the learning of skills is not something we can leave up to a lucky discovery. On the other hand, the teacher-directed art activity is often designed around the learning or practice of a skill. However, in this case, the skill is not learned within the context of a meaningful project, but rather as an unconnected physical exercise, an extraneous piece of information not rooted in a valuable process. Understand, skill acquisition is fantastically important; children without skills cannot give concrete form to their thoughts, expressions, or feelings. However, this does not mean that skill acquisition should be taught as an end in itself or as the sole objective of a teacher-directed art activity. Skill acquisition is part of and, at the same time, a by-product of the process. In other words, for children to learn the skills needed to actively take part in artistic experiences, skill acquisition should be embedded in meaningful experience. This is accomplished by teaching skills in conjunction with the formulation of individual expression or when observation exposes a child's need or desire to use media in a particular fashion to pursue form (Lowenfeld and Brittain 1987).

The common and continuous use of these erroneous approaches leaves educators unable to identify or understand their part in children's artistic endeavours. Unaware, many carry-on either not getting involved in children's art making or getting involved only to over-direct the activity.

When we stand back, fail to participate in the child's art experiences, hesitate to gently intervene, or only offer simple sensory or teacher-directed activities that deny the opportunity to engage in a beneficial process, we forfeit any chance of real artistic development. The adults' role is just as crucial in the artistic development of children as it is in the other areas of a child's development. Kolbe (1993) concluded that by engaging in communication and by using appropriate intervention, educators perform a fundamental function in the artistic growth of young children. Additionally, over a nine-month period in a pre-school class, Kindler (1995: 14) observed that the art area was rarely used, and when it was used, the child's experience did not stretch beyond making a few marks. Kindler (ibid.: 14) found:

> Only when a parent or a teacher stayed with a child and became involved in a dialogue related to actions that the child was performing, did the child seem inclined to truly explore the available materials and tools, or to experiment with their use.

If we want children to connect with art's educational potential, educators need to sensitively intervene, be fully involved, and, in many cases, join the child on their artistic journey (Brittain 1979; Eglinton 2002; Kindler 1995; Kolbe 1993).

In our comprehensive art model, the educator plays a major role by energising artistic experiences through interactions with the child, which include dialogue, motivation, observation, and documentation. These interactions enable the child to both affect, and be affected by the process. Artistic experiences and the holistic model discussed throughout the remainder of Part I, and the artistic experiences offered in Part II require the total and active involvement of the educators in the children's artistic education.

LEARNING IN THE PROCESS: ART MAKING EXPERIENCES

Since we have already ascertained that the non-interventionist, materials approach, and the teacher-directed art activity are ineffective, we now turn our attention to positive art experiences. Accordingly, we ask, what types of art experiences are appropriate, educational, and beneficial?

The remainder of this chapter explores art making; however, because our model is holistic, references are repeatedly made to the other two forms of art experience: aesthetic experiences and encounters with art. Appreciate, that because of the model's interrelated structure, the basic ideas and elements described in this chapter, including motivation and dialogue, are relevant to all three forms of experience. In fact, motivation and dialogue, we will soon see, are integral elements of the model. See Chapter 3 for aesthetic experiences and encounters with art.

Art activities vs. art making experiences

Gaspar (1995) makes a distinction between art making experiences and 'fabrication activities'. Fabrication Gaspar (ibid.: 46) defines as 'to make or build by joining parts; to construct'. This differentiation is important; a simple activity or fabrication activity, similar to the teacher-directed method previously described, fails to realise art's potential, and instead occupies children with the fabrication of a teacher-driven model. Some educators offer fabrication activities thinking the children are engaging in an art experience without seeing the difference. We approach art with good intentions, offer what seem to be sound educational activities, but unfortunately, many of the activities do not come close to an art making experience. In fact, the difference between an art making experience and a simple art activity is immense. With this in mind, we ask three important questions: when is an art activity an art making experience? How can we make an art activity into an art making experience? Finally, what does a sound art making experience include? (These questions, particularly the first one, are inspired by Gaspar's (1995: 46) similar queries, and have been adapted for our purposes.)

An art making experience

To answer the first question, an art activity is an art making experience when it has a valuable process that, in some way, affects the child and, at the same time, allows the child to affect or transform it. What is more, perhaps synonymously, true art making experiences are dynamic: one experience generates another experience. Art making experiences will always include the elements of dialogue and motivation, and art making experiences are flexible, based on the child's needs, and constantly supported by the teacher. An art activity, on the other hand, does not include an educational process; in a typical art activity, a child can usually follow the steps and get from A to B without the slightest change to their development. An art activity, for example, might require a child to fabricate a pre-determined product, by simply gluing already cut fabric to a pre-made pattern. The result is known, children cannot change the procedure; furthermore, the process or steps followed to complete the product do not beneficially affect the child. If there is no change to the child, if discoveries are not made, if the experience remains unaffected and ends without leading to anything else, then there was no valuable process, and without a valuable process, educators can be sure they did not have an art experience. On the other hand, if the activity affected the child, led to a discovery, and generated excitement; and, in addition, if the child was able to affect the course of the activity by applying the new knowledge gained in the form of either an extended or new project then you almost certainly just had an art experience.

To answer the second question, how to make an art activity into an art making experience, Szyba (1999: 16) suggests choosing art making experiences the same way experts choose appropriate toys; toys should be 'open-ended', there should be numerous possibilities for their use, and they should encourage imaginative growth, investigation, and active learning. This is a helpful comparison; if we wish to offer both a valuable process and dynamic experiences, we need to engage in lessons that can lead us to any number of conclusions. One way of doing this is by trying our best not to enter into the experience with a product in mind. Understandably, this is difficult; some of us may argue that it is quite hard to think about creating something without envisioning the resulting form; however, in the case of art teaching we have to 'let the process in' – allow the process to take us to any number of ends. Keep in mind, however, that this does not mean we step aside as teachers and, say, let the media teach. Getting the most from the process requires the active participation of both the educator and the child. As the child moves through the process, the teacher recognises, points out, and expands on the child's discoveries. The child and teacher are thought of as colleagues searching, exploring, flowing with, and at the same time guiding the experience.

In Part II of this book, the art experiences do have titles, many of these titles indicating a pre-determined result; this is because we need objectives, goals, aims, a structure or framework; if we do not plan, we risk sacrificing all of art's educational attributes. Schaefer and Cole (1990: 5–6) point out that 'structure' can simply mean 'a constant awareness in the teacher's mind of the underlying principles of a designed curriculum'. It is necessary to remember that a plan is a sketch: malleable, adaptable, and flexible. The indicated product is a tangible remnant of the voyage; when we are mindful of this, we open up to the possibilities within the process. In fact, we know we have had an actual art making experience when we completely lose ourselves in the journey, and finish with a product that looks nothing like what we had originally envisioned.

With a better idea of the difference between a simple art activity and an art making experience, we look closely at the third question: what does a sound art making experience include?

Art making experiences will always include a process that involves the child in any number of developmental and growth experiences. Appropriate art making experiences offer one or more of the following:

- Problem-solving opportunities including, but not limited to, problems relating to the use of materials, construction, placement, the giving of shape to feelings, ideas, experiences, or figuring out how best to communicate thoughts.
- The opportunity for personal expression, the communication of subjective perceptions, the clarifying of undefined feelings or thoughts.
- Time for sensory exploration, exploration of media, the active seeking and extracting of information from both the natural and constructed environment.
- Time for skill development, the process of gaining control over media, the use of materials in the expression of form.

• Support in the development of symbolic form, the creation and de-coding of symbols, using symbols to communicate personal ideas, thoughts, feelings, experiences, and using symbols to make sense of the environment.

Finally, and very important, art making experiences must be both meaningful and integrated into the child's total learning experience; in order for this to happen we need to refrain from offering isolated irrelevant product-oriented activities. All sound art experiences, including aesthetic experiences and encounters with art, are not isolated incidents, they stem from, among numerous other factors, continuous dialogue and motivation, a child's prior knowledge, preceding artistic experiences, and the like. The rest of this chapter and the remainder of Part I explore the idea of integrated, meaningful, and relevant art experiences.

We noted earlier another difference between art activities and art making experiences, specifically that art making experiences, and indeed all forms of artistic experience including aesthetic experiences and encounters with art, are dynamic: the process continuously leading us to new uncharted territory – learning sparking further learning. However, this cycle does not just happen; educators are required to use continuous *motivation* and *dialogue*, integral elements in our holistic model, to propel art's dynamic nature. Figure 2.1 illustrates how and where motivation and dialogue fit in the model.

Motivation

A motive is something that encourages or generates action. To motivate is to provoke or incite interest. In order to support art learning, relevant, active, and multi-sensory motivation is vital. Some believe that young children are

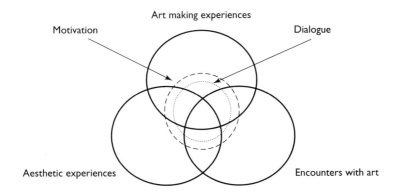

Figure 2.1   All art experiences are dynamic, yet we need to propel this active nature; two elements we use to fuel experiences are motivation and dialogue. Motivation and dialogue happen throughout experiences, they help sustain and generate new experiences. The relationship between all of the elements is highly interrelated

'self-motivated' or that art materials alone will stimulate the child into action. While this belief is to some degree true, a total submission to its possibility usually results in the non-interventionist approach to art teaching – staff take a back seat and let enthusiasm for media guide the experience. As already pointed out, the exploration of media, while a fine initial encounter, is not enough. The construction of personal expression into form, skill development, and cognitive, aesthetic, and perceptual growth needs fostering. We cannot assume for one minute that children will be motivated to express their ideas simply because they enjoy touching clay. For both dynamic experiences and a child's active and total submersion in the process, motivation is required throughout the experience. Motivation at the beginning serves as the initial 'spark', during the experience it offers feedback and helps regenerate involvement, at the end it promotes reflection and stimulates further experiences.

Types of motivation

Motivation in artistic experiences takes many forms, including inspiration, enthusiasm, or excitement. It can be found in anything from a snowstorm, to a song, to a delicious dessert. A highly adaptable element, motivation can be the spark that ignites experience, it can be an encounter with art, an aesthetic experience, or the art making experience itself – motivation, educators will find, is the most malleable component of artistic experiences.

Ways to motivate children include using:

- The children's own work – first, children's artwork, we discovered, develops within the process. This process is very motivating, when children see their art forming they are stimulated by this concrete expression, and are driven to further creation. Second, have children reflect on previous experiences, these past creations serve as a starting point for new creations (it also enables children to see a connection between past and present knowledge).
- Art encounters – use art history, cultural studies, participation in the art world to spark personal form and expression (see Chapter 3 for encounters with art).
- Aesthetic experiences – let experiences with beauty lead children into further explorations with the natural and constructed environment (see Chapter 3 for aesthetic experiences).
- Books and stories – use books to explore art elements, expressions, symbols. The educator can do an author study, a thematic study, or a stylistic study (in each case experiences are built around an author, theme, or artistic style).
- The natural environment – nature offers us unlimited inspiration, from massive thunderstorms, to furry animals, to the smallest grain of sand. Show children how nature can stir and move them; teaching children how to actively observe and perceive will awaken children to nature's fantastic motivational promise. Remember, although children's imaginations are vivid, much of this internal world is a result of external observation and experience.

- The constructed environment – look at the made world, explore the colours and patterns, and compare it to the natural world. Try to find inspiration in everyday objects; seek the complex in the simple.
- Documentation – writing down children's comments and collecting their concrete expressions serve as the motivation for further creations (see Chapter 4 for documentation).
- Materials – as an initial exploratory experience art materials can be incredibly motivating. Try to include this initial exploration time into every art making experience. In addition, sometimes the simple act of caring for or preparing materials is motivating; filling the paint pots thrills even the adults.
- The educator – the educator is the most important motivating force in the learning environment. An educator's attitude towards art and the desire to explore and discover serve as a model for the children. If educators lose themselves in art, the children will be motivated to do the same; enthusiasm is contagious. The educator creates learning situations, points out problems, and encourages perceptual growth – these are all motivational functions.
- Exhibitions and collections of small objects – having displays of found (both natural and human made) objects are necessary motivational tools in any art learning setting. Microscopes and magnifying glasses should be part of the collection if genuine discovery is an objective.
- Imagination and fantasy – drawing on children's rich imagination triggers infinite experiences. A child's inner world is so spectacularly huge it could literally stimulate and motivate years and years of art experiences.
- Art games – any subject becomes exciting when we learn it through fun. Matching and sorting games motivate learning about the formal elements of art, while physical games can trigger off energetic painting and sculpture.
- Spontaneous events – during the course of the day any number of extraordinary things can happen that give rise to the stimulation of art making experiences. For example, a snowfall, a child's birthday, the birth of a new brother or sister.
- Play – children naturally learn through play. Use play to motivate an art experience such as making textiles for the house area. Or use play as a motivational tool in art history, children can pretend to be part of a painting, role play going to an art gallery, or being an artist in a studio; the ideas are endless.
- Holidays – holidays offer incredible motivation to fantastic art making. Strive for personal expression and be careful not to fall prey to the stereotypical holiday crafts.
- Multi-sensory – use the senses to motivate, and at the same time, remember, motivation should take place through the senses. The more senses we can stimulate, the more the child can draw from and be excited by the experience. Use dialogue, touchy-feely boxes, texture walls, and hands-on experiences to stimulate art learning. A multi-sensory approach should be part of all positive motivation.

- Physical activity – motivate children by asking them to observe how we run, jump, and walk. Ask what muscles are being used, how we feel, smell, and look when we jump, feel hot, chase the ball. Teach the children to observe each other's physical features and remarkable feats. Show children how these observations can stimulate art making experiences.
- Memory – enable children to get and stay inspired by helping them recall both familiar and special events (from eating breakfast to going to the zoo). Bring in all the senses, help children relive the event, encourage them to respond visually.

The number of motivational ideas is endless. Inside the minutes of any chosen hour inspirational opportunities continuously present themselves; whether we grab hold of these opportunities depends upon our ability to recognise them. As educators, when we become alert to stimulating material, moments, and chances, and open ourselves up to the vast quantities of motivation residing in our everyday world we will never be short of ideas to ignite and perpetuate artistic experiences.

Discussion and dialogue

Discussion or dialogue, the terms are used here interchangeably, is an essential and integral part of all art experiences. It can motivate, guide, encourage, provide vital feedback, extend, and/or intensify involvement in the process. Similar to motivation, continuous dialogue is necessary to support art's active character; it stimulates and helps generate experience. Constructive dialogue is entirely dependent on teacher intervention for its implementation and facilitation. It is important that we know how and when to use it if we are to capitalise on its educational value.

Dialogue as motivation

Dialogue serves as an excellent motivational tool. Educators can remind children of previous experiences, help them recall memories, and encourage them to verbalise prior knowledge, feelings, and ideas. When using dialogue as a motivational tool, educators should ask questions that address perceptual, sensory, and personal issues. For example, if prompting children to remember a trip to the zoo, questions can range from 'What was the weather like?' to 'What was your favourite part of the day?' to 'What colour were the bears?' If wanting children to respond and think about an object, person, or idea that is the focus of a particular art experience, teachers might ask 'What does the fabric (person, animal, painting . . .) feel like?' or 'How does mummy (new sister Sue, this tree . . .) move (sleep, talk . . .)?'

Throughout an experience dialogue continues to motivate children. This motivation can come in the form of praise, it can be used to jog perceptual memories, or sometimes just having a dialogue is motivating enough for children to carry on creating with enthusiasm. After a hands-on (usually the fashioning of form) part of an experience, motivational dialogue continues as praise and as a form of feedback (see following sections). When using dialogue to motivate, use rich, expressive words, teach children descriptive words, talk about how objects or experiences feel, look, taste, smell, sound.

Dialogue as praise

Praise is an incredibly complicated variety of dialogue. Educators need to put a lot of thought into how, when, and why they offer children praise. Observation reveals that children are perceptive and can usually tell if adults are being thoughtful and sincere in their comments.

It is important that praise is offered throughout artistic experiences. In the beginning of an experience, praise children for taking part in initial dialogue, for using their senses, for noticing slight perceptual differences, for being active or aware. By praising initial dialogue, children see it as a vital part of the total experience. If making art, during the hands-on stage, it is important not to offer praise unthinkingly or too continuously. When praise is continuous, the tone begins to sound monotonous, the words lose their power, and the experience loses its meaningfulness.

Praise must be carefully considered. Children need to see an interested adult, someone involved, who looks and makes comments that are individualised and thoughtful. Praise such as 'good work' offers children little in the way of individual encouragement or positive reinforcement; whereas, a comment such as 'I really like that colour you mixed! How did you do it?' is not only personalised, it also engages the child in dialogue. An educator's praise should be suited to the child's developmental level. For example, praising a child in the random scribbling stage, the educator might comment on the kinaesthetic involvement or, if a child is in the schematic stage, comments may address issues of representation.

After a hands-on part of an experience, any praise regarding the product should stress and highlight the process. For example, instead of saying 'I like the colour you painted the sky', say 'I thought it was great the way you mixed the white and blue to get the colour for your sky'. Praise is not only used to encourage children, it is also a wonderful tool for providing feedback and for helping children reflect on their own artistic processes. Finally, when using praise, employ words that describe the process and elements of art such as line, shape, colour, paint mixing, pounding the clay, tearing paper. For example, 'I think it is great the way you have drawn that line using a blue crayon.' Refer to Table 3.2 for the art elements and principles of art.

Dialogue as feedback

Art constantly generates visual feedback; dialogue, however, can greatly enhance and intensify this feedback. Though often disguised as praise, feedback comes in many forms; educators should offer feedback throughout the entire art experience. While some feedback, such as 'You are doing that wrong', is negative; other feedback is positive and constructive. Positive constructive feedback highlights the positive features of the work and comments on the process, objective, or skill being assessed. A statement such as 'The way you cut that paper is perfect' is typical of positive constructive feedback. Drummond *et al.* (1992), in describing four different types of feedback, consider positive constructive feedback, as exemplified above, as the most productive type. With this type of feedback children see what they have successfully accomplished, and what they need to be attempting. Other examples of positive constructive feedback include, for example, 'That is the correct way to hold your paintbrush, now you can paint more beautiful pictures!' or 'It looks like the lines you are drawing are dancing, I think it is wonderful the way you can draw lines to the music we are listening to.'

Keep in mind any feedback, regardless of intention, can be interpreted as either negative or positive. It is the educator's responsibility to articulate feedback so that it will be interpreted as positive and encouraging. We learn and grow from our experiences through feedback, and, for that reason, adults need to be sensitive to how they administer it. Unconstructive negative feedback offers nothing in the way of growth and will only serve to hinder artistic progress, whereas positive constructive feedback can significantly enrich and extend the child's artistic experience. When providing feedback, concentrate on vocabulary that highlights the art process.

Dialogue as instruction

When the aim is to offer process-driven art experiences, meaningful to the child and full of possibility, some may find it difficult to imagine how and when instructions fit into the experience. Yet we know from practice that educators must give instructions and offer advice if we want to meet goals, objectives, and enable children to establish the skills they need to express themselves effectively. Moreover, with the implementation of the early learning goals, it is no longer possible to ignore teaching art. Where sequential, valuable, and sound art experiences are desired, instructions are inevitable. The question now is, how can we offer needed instructions yet still promote process-driven experiences? The answer is quite straightforward. We must offer instructions and learn that it is *how* we give instruction that will determine whether children find them confining or gently guiding and motivating.

From the beginning, allow children to make their own decisions within each step of the process; doing this will keep the experience from becoming prescribed and will help maintain an emphasis on the process. For example, if children are painting, give children a choice of paper size or if children are using clay, allow them to determine what wooden tools they would like to employ. Open up the possibilities, allow for choice, and generate opportunities for individual expression within each step. Instructions and structure do not mean a teacher-directed constricting experience. Give instructions using goals as a guide, but with the process and the children's development as priority. When giving instructions refer to art media and equipment by the proper terminology, and frequently repeat the names of tools and materials so children have a chance to hear and remember them.

Dialogue as a way of extending the experience

Continuous dialogue serves to extend art experiences. Throughout the entire experience, educators should use dialogue as a way to help children learn from the process, recognise and solve problems, apply new discoveries, facilitate reflection, and expand their thinking. During the process children will encounter problems ranging from skill limitations to expressional concerns; using discussion as a tool, adults can help children recognise artistic challenges and aid in finding subsequent solutions. What is more, it is during the process that new ideas arise, experiments and discoveries take place, and new constructs are made. Educators should seize upon these occasions and, using active dialogue, expand the given experience into further explorations and future artistic endeavours. Schaefer and Cole (1990: 6) refer to 'teachable moments' as moments where, with the curriculum goals in mind, the adult presents further learning opportunities. During the process children constantly present us with teachable moments, every challenge they encounter, every discovery they make, every exploration allows for the possibility of lengthening, extending, and branching out the experience. If we use dialogue to seek out and capitalise on these fantastic moments, one artistic experience could lead to hundreds.

Dialogue, regardless of its role in the experience, should always be geared to a child's stage of development (for other references, see Seefeldt 1995). In the early scribbling stage keep dialogue to kinaesthetic and sensory issues, remark on how wonderfully children can swing their arms, how the crayon feels, what the clay smells like (ibid.). When children can control their scribbles, comment on how well they control the pen, how interesting the pattern is they created, or challenge them to control a more difficult material such as paint. When children begin to name their scribbles, use the opportunity to extend their perceptions and subsequent symbols. If the child draws and names it 'cat', extend their thinking, ask how the cat feels, how the cat walks, what noises the cat makes. Challenge children in the schematic stage on all counts. Use dialogue to extend their experience, expand perceptual awareness, and help them make their expression tangible (ibid.).

During all stages of children's development, discussion should be rich in expressive vocabulary and accurate in terminology. Furthermore, dialogue should maintain the open-endedness necessary for an exciting interchange between the educator and child. This is done by asking children to analyse, describe, solve, and discover, and by refraining from asking yes or no questions such as 'Did you use paint?' Yes or no questions are closed and do nothing to extend or enrich the process. On the other hand, by encouraging children to reflect on the process, asking questions that demand thought and allow for personal input, offering children a chance to nurture their own expression through discussion, and promoting the exchange of ideas, an educator brings the process to life, and helps drive art's dynamic force (Chapman 1978).

Before moving on to look at the other forms of art experience, specifically, aesthetic experiences and encounters with art, it is necessary to reiterate a key point. While in this book (for simplicity) the components that make up a comprehensive art programme, and indeed artistic experience, are presented in a somewhat separated manner, in practice, all the elements are connected and interrelated. In proper early childhood art methodology, the distinction between art making (including the required motivation and dialogue), aesthetic experiences, and encounters with art is very difficult to make. Art making experiences, for example, will always include a motivational component, and sometimes this motivation takes the form of a short aesthetic experience. Alternatively, encounters with works of art will often serve as the motivation in an art making experience or, sometimes, an encounter with a work of art will in fact be the art experience itself. Refer to Figure 2.1 to see the relationship between all of the components.

Chapter 3

The process continues:

Aesthetic experiences and encounters with art

This chapter explores aesthetic experiences and encounters with art. As illustrated in Figures 1.1 and 2.1, both a comprehensive art programme and artistic experiences are not limited to making art, also integrated is a multitude of aesthetic experiences as well as encounters with art.

Gaspar (1995) describes types of art experiences in early childhood art. One is the traditional experience in the sense that it includes the use of art media in the creation of a tangible object. Another involves using the senses to carefully observe, feel, see, or hear; Gaspar (ibid.: 46) refers to these as 'aesthetic experiences, . . . experiences of beauty'. We look closer at aesthetic experiences in a moment, but first we take the liberty here of adding to Gaspar's list another type of artistic experience, called *encountering art*. This type of experience includes not only looking at, reflecting upon, and growing from art's past, present, and future, but it also incorporates, for example, exposure to crafts, artists, artifacts, and art from diverse cultures.

AESTHETIC EXPERIENCES

Aesthetic experiences, a variety of artistic experience and a necessary part of any early years art programme, foster in children a deeper perceptual understanding of the world, and, at times, serve to bridge and connect art making and encounters with art. Aesthetic experiences contribute to and alter children's knowledge of the world, add to and intensify perceptions and experiences, guide children in subsequent encounters with works of art, and awaken children to the beauty in everyday experiences and objects. Intrigued, many might now be wondering, what are aesthetic experiences? To answer that question we first need to understand the word aesthetic – a complex, and, to some educators, unapproachable word.

As indicated in Chapter 1, those involved in early years art often point out the difference between aesthetics as a noun, which refers to a branch of philosophy concerned with the nature of art, and aesthetics as an adjective which means capable of or concerned with an appreciation of beauty (Hagaman 1990; Herberholz and Hanson 1995). While, discipline-based art education (DBAE) draws on the discipline of aesthetics as a branch of philosophy, in early childhood we are concerned with the word aesthetics as an adjective. Studying aesthetics as a subject, Herberholz and Hanson (1995) argue, is too complex for the early years; and further reason that philosophical aesthetic issues are often, nevertheless, touched upon during encounters with art. Questions such as 'What is art?', 'Is a dog art?' are easily worked into a dialogue concerning works of art. Hagaman (1990), though indicating that it is possible on some level to teach aesthetics as a philosophy to children, also believes it should be combined and blended into art making, art history, and art criticism rather than taught as a separate discipline. This book agrees with the literature and merges the teaching of aesthetics as a noun or discipline into our encounters with art. In doing so, we are left with the word aesthetics as an adjective – capable of or concerned with an appreciation of beauty. What does this mean in early childhood art? Again, what are aesthetic experiences?

We established in Chapter 1 that we connect with the environment through the senses; stimulation, inspiration, and information are extracted from the environment through the senses. The senses are the channels through which we learn. However, we discovered young children need to learn how to use the senses actively to select, truly see, hear, observe, distinguish, and feel. Aesthetic experiences do just this, they awaken children's senses to the world around them, facilitate discovery, examination, and enable children to see and appreciate the beauty in not just a work of art or awe-inspiring landscape, but also in, for example, a dried-up leaf, in the inside of a banana peel, or even a colourful pile of refuse.

Some believe aesthetic experiences are experiences that are pleasurable in themselves offering no extrinsic reward such as money or fame; the value of the experience is 'intrinsic' (Feeney and Moravcik 1987: 7; Logan 1955). An example of this type of aesthetic experience occurs as you sit on a beach, feel the hot sand beneath your body, feel a breeze over your face, hear the waves, take in the smell of the ocean. For that one moment all of your senses are open, the experience does not pay you, but it impresses you, if only for a few seconds. In another example, sometimes making art is an aesthetic experience. Caught in a flow, body and mind working together, submerged in the process; the individual is aware of the experience, senses are awakened, the experience itself is of value. In a slightly differing interpretation, Gaspar (1995: 46) describes an aesthetic experience as using the senses, and responding through a process called 'guided looking'. Giving children the opportunity to reflect and react to what they see, hear, or feel, Gaspar believes, is the difference between passively taking something in through the senses and having an aesthetic experience. In this explanation, adults enable children, through careful and thoughtful questioning, to respond to their senses.

There are various interpretations of aesthetic experiences, yet a close reading uncovers a similar base. Feeney and Moravcik (1987: 7) concluded most descriptions of aesthetic experience include 'the capacity to perceive, respond, and be sensitive to the natural environment and to human creations'. We add that aesthetic experiences require an awareness and full absorption of the individual in the experience. With this addition, we form our own definition of aesthetic experiences as:

> Intrinsically valuable sensory experiences that absorb us, awaken us, and elicit a response and an understanding of beauty found in both the natural and constructed environment.

Aesthetic experiences cultivate observation and reflection, they give children a base for looking at and responding to works of art, they bring artistic thinking and looking into everyday living. Aesthetic experiences encourage children to expand their already natural sense of wonder, and while not engaged in for material ends, aesthetic experiences do often lead to art making. The power of some experiences is so consuming, children are naturally compelled to respond both verbally and visually.

It must be remembered that although children approach the world with senses wide open and come equipped with a natural desire to explore, it is up to educators to show children how, what, where, and when to use the senses with awareness, discernment, and understanding (Gaspar 1995). It is our job to put in their path objects of wonder, beauty, and awe, to point out the brilliance in the everyday, to notice the unnoticeable, to seek subtlety in the obvious, to be inspired by ordinary events, or sense the unfamiliar in the familiar. Ask children to respond and encourage children to take an active role in their experience (ibid.).

It is unnecessary to offer a specified time to engage in aesthetic experiences, for opportunities to partake in these experiences present themselves every moment – whether we act on them or not depends on our own perceptual sensitivity and awareness. In Chapter 2 we learned that sometimes an aesthetic experience is used as a type of motivation, or that sometimes it will be an art experience in itself. Indeed, when and how aesthetic experiences are used is entirely up to the educator. However, keep in mind that aesthetic experiences are a vital component of our comprehensive model and need to be participated in, optimistically speaking, on a daily basis, but, realistically, on a regular basis. Educators must ensure children have opportunities to engage in all forms of art experience on an equal basis: children should have as many aesthetic experiences as they do art making experiences, as many encountering art experiences as they do aesthetic experiences, and so forth. The following section offers staff some ideas for aesthetic experiences.

Ideas for aesthetic experiences

- Think nature – for example, study a leaf, look at the veins, the colour, the colours inside those colours, the shape, the shapes within the shape, the microscopic lines, feel the texture, look for pattern, and respond to how it feels, looks, smells. Let it fly through the air, watch it sail and land, bring it inside the classroom, does it belong inside? Does it look different inside than outside? Wet it down, look at the colour change, dry it out, smell the leaf when it is wet, dry, as it decomposes, note any changes. Look at the stem, why is it different? How does it feel? Look at the leaf under a microscope, look at the leaf from far away; always elicit a response, encourage observation and personal identification with the object or event.

- Become an object – help children identify with and see the wonder in objects by pretending to be that object. Facilitate use of the senses by asking children to sound, feel, look, possibly smell and even taste like an everyday object. Ask children, for example, to become an orange. What shape would they be? Where would they live? What would their texture feel like? How would they react when a big hand grabbed them from a bowl? How would they unpeel? Have children role play being that object.

  Other examples: have children become a house. How big would they be? What colour would they be? Would they taste like anything? What would they feel like? Can they make their bodies look like a house? Ask children to be a pair of glasses. What shape are they? Where do they stay? Are they in a case, on a nose, on someone's head? What colour are they? Enable children to identify with objects, learn the object's design; feel, see, touch, experience the object; show them the beauty of simple natural or human made creations.

- Go shopping – take advantage of a trip to the shop to awaken and elicit aesthetic response. Go to the food shop and notice the colours of the vegetables, the smell of the cheeses, and the feel of the fruits. Glide through the frozen food section, does it feel cooler? Appear colder? Look at packaging; notice the shapes and colours of the wrappers and boxes. What do we want to buy? What are we drawn to? Can we smell through boxes? Can we tell what something tastes like from the package?

  Take children out into the world, let them aesthetically experience what we would sometimes cast off as an errand or chore. Make it an event, a sensory extravaganza. Encourage responses, and take advantage of the journey both to and from the shop or point of destination to have a multitude of aesthetic experiences.

- Eat dinner – make even the most basic events aesthetic ones. In this case, an event of survival offers hundreds of opportunities for aesthetic experiences. Start with setting the table; it is an event in itself. Enable children to make aesthetic choices, let them pick out the tablecloth, shine the spoons, fold the napkins. When food arrives, examine the colours, the way orange carrots look next to green beans, move them, do they look different next to the beets? Does the orange colour change? What about the way the potatoes lie on top of each other, do they change shape if you separate them? Feel the texture of the fish, meat, chicken, vegetable, pudding, is it soft? What about the taste?

Can it be described? Can the taste be seen in the texture? Encourage children to taste every bite, feel every chew, and take in all of the aromas.

- Take a walk – the possibilities are endless. Before embarking, have some objectives in mind, or let nature be your guide. Study the dirt beneath your feet, listen to the sound of your steps, smell the air, feel the temperature. Touch, smell, see, and respond to trees, grass, mud, sand, rocks. Look up at the clouds, look directly in front of you, see what is on either side of you. If you are in an urban environment, take in the noise, listen for birds, differentiate the aromas, and strain to hear your steps. The simple act of taking a walk can lead to possibilities never imagined.

- Sit in the sun – or wind or shade . . . encourage children to be aware of just 'being'. Using the wind as an example, close your eyes and feel the bench, ground, sand underneath you. Is it hard? Soft? Feel the wind on your body. Where does the wind touch your body? How do you know? What does it feel like? Can you hear the wind? Taste it? Open your eyes. Can you see the wind? Does it move? What colour is it? Can we see the impression wind leaves? Does the wind change objects? Does it change us? Does it make our hair look funny? Does it make us feel cold? Look in the sky, how does the wind affect the sky? The clouds? Use this type of questioning to awaken children to their surroundings, and to the impact of the surroundings on their senses.

- Watch the rain – actively experience rain. From indoors, watch the sky, the clouds, do they move? What colour is the sky? What colour are the clouds? What colour are the raindrops? Can we see each one separately? What would they feel like if they landed on us? Hard? Soft? Tickly? What would raindrops taste like? Do they have a smell? What about the ground, does it change colour when it gets wet? Does the grass, dirt, or sand look different?

  If you are caught outside in the rain, do not run indoors, instead take a minute to 'be'. Feel the drops on your body, the wet beneath your feet. What do raindrops feel like when they land on us? What do they taste like? Can we smell rain? Run through the rain, does it feel different now? Can we dodge the raindrops? Can we follow one raindrop with our eyes from the sky to the ground? Does everything look different when it is wet? Do our faces look different when they are wet? Do we feel different? Encourage children to get lost in the moment.

- Look out of the window – prompt children to take a moment to stand at the window. Look through the glass, what do you see? Do you see the glass? Do you see outside? Do you see both at once? Can you smell the outside through the glass? Can you feel how hot or cold it is outside? Can you see temperature? How much can you see from the window? Can you see all around you, what is in front and behind you? If it just rained, can you imagine what it smells like? If you spot a flower, can you smell it from here? Can you think of its scent? Can we touch what we see? What do we think the grass, dirt, tree feels like? Go to the window often, try to experience the outside through glass; compare it to experiencing it without the barrier.

- Examine your body – choose a part of the body and explore it in detail. For example, encourage children to look at their hands; get absorbed in the knuckles, fingernails, veins. Study and respond to the shape, look at the shapes inside the main shape. Search and feel for texture, look for patterns in the lines, and in the overall form. Look for cuts and bruises, and at the colour of the skin. Is the colour smooth and even? Is the colour on the outside the same as the colour of your palms? Make a fist, squeeze, how does it feel?

  Show us what it looks like. Loosen your hands and make them go limp. How do they feel now? Do they look bigger or smaller than when they were in a fist? Smell your hands. What do they smell like? Food? Soap? Nothing? Look at your palms, travel along the lines. Clap your hands together. Clap them hard and soft. Can you feel the difference? Hear the difference? Can you make a sound using just one hand? Explore every part of the body. Look at surface, form, movement. Study the body as you would an object, experience it aesthetically.

- Listen to music – experience music through all of the senses. First, hear it. How does it sound? Fast, slow, loud, soft? Dance to it, move your whole body. Try your best to feel it. Can you see it? What colour would it be? Would it be multi-coloured? Would it be bright or dark? Can you taste it? Would this music taste sweet, crunchy, or chewy? Can you smell this music? Does it smell like flowers? Sour milk? Encourage children to cross and connect their senses, elicit their response; also allow them to get lost in the music, become absorbed. Repeat this type of experience using other typically visual, audible, tactile media. For example, ask children to hear a painting, imagine the taste of fabric or texture, visualise sound. This connection heightens and sharpens perception, which, in turn, can enhance subsequent aesthetic experiences.

See Table 3.1 for additional aesthetic experiences.

Chances to engage in aesthetic experiences are literally endless; true to the dynamic nature of artistic experience, aesthetic experiences will prompt further learning and investigation. The more we allow these experiences to infiltrate our daily existence, the more we nurture the artistic education of young children, and lay the foundation for a life driven by active discovery, reflection, and response; in short, a life rich in aesthetic understanding. The remainder of this chapter looks at the third type of art experience, and indispensable element in our holistic model, called *encounters with art*.

ENCOUNTERING ART

Feeney and Moravcik (1987: 8) distinguish between two approaches in art education. The first they refer to as '*studio-oriented*'; this approach places emphasis

Table 3.1 Short aesthetic experiences

Experience
Jump and run – get lost in the moment, feel every muscle, try to hear your heart beat.
Experience silence – close your eyes, and listen to the sound of nothing. Can you hear it? Become absorbed in it.
Get dressed up – choose fabrics of personally pleasing colours, experience the clothes falling over your shoulders, the sound of the zips, and the feel of the various textures.
Water a plant – notice colour changes, watch the water as it splashes off leaves and is sucked into the dirt.
Wash your hands – truly experience this ordinary task. Awaken the senses to the feel of the cool water, the foam of the soap. Build up lather, smell the aroma, make many bubbles, rub your hands together, rinse and watch the foam run off your fingertips.
Study your favourite object – what is so special about your favourite blanket, doll, toy car? Experience your beloved possession, what colour is it? How does it feel? What does it sound like? Does it have a smell? How does it move? Become immersed in its characteristics.
Build with blocks – take a moment to build a tower. Work slowly, feel the wooden blocks in your hand, keep it balanced, lose yourself in the process. Knock it down, watch the building crumble, the blocks hit the ground; listen to the crash.
Watch a bird fly – or dog run, or horse jump, or turtle crawl. Try to feel what they are feeling, the ground pounding beneath them or the air through their wings.
Take a train ride – a boat ride, a bicycle ride, a bus ride, a car trip; smell and taste the air, feel vibrations and speed, take in the colours as they pass by, look for patterns in the moving landscape. Listen for rhythm in the sound of the engine, turn of the pedals, or the click and clank of the wheels on the track.

on making art, and, as the authors point out, is common practice in early childhood education. Proponents of this style believe children should *not* encounter works of art; they reason 'it is inappropriate to inflict adult interpretations of beauty on children because self-expression will be stifled and willingness to take risks diminished' (ibid.: 8). The authors suggest this way of thinking leads to a child's limited contact with works of art and, subsequently, 'education for aesthetic development is delayed' (ibid.). The other method, described by Feeney and Moravcik, is more holistic and wide-ranging; it sees art education as more than just a series of art making activities. In this approach, children *are* offered encounters with works of art. The belief is '[c]hildren's response to art and an environment rich in beauty of all kinds is considered an integral part of learning about the arts' (ibid.). Many support this inclusive approach, and different methods have been initiated for the teaching of a more complete art education including, the Getty Center for Education in the Arts' discipline-based art education (1985), and Project Zero's Arts PROPEL, see Gardner (1989).

The differing opinions between those who support a production based art education and those who promote a more far-reaching approach prompt investigation into whether or not young children should be actively encountering and discussing great cultural and artistic achievements. Hence we ask, is early childhood an appropriate time for children to encounter art?

A review of the literature indicates that early childhood is an excellent time to provide children with art opportunities that extend far past fabrication or production activities (Colbert 1995; Cole and Schaefer 1990; Feeney and Moravcik 1987; Herberholz and Hanson, 1995; Honigman and Bhavnagri 1998; Kerlavage 1995; Schaefer and Cole 1990; Schiller 1995). Feeney and Moravcik (1987) point out that in early childhood we establish children's aesthetic base upon which further art experiences are built. Encounters with art connect children to their past, encourage both cultural identification and awareness, and offer children the chance to contribute to, partake in, and draw from the world's huge store of cultural and artistic treasures. A report by the Getty Center for Education in the Arts (1985: 4) revealed art would remain a subordinate subject and would not 'reach its full potential until schools approach it more substantively'. Eisner (1985: 64) states, 'the arts represent the highest of human achievements to which students should have access'; an arts programme based solely on production denies children this access, perpetuates the unfortunate notion that art is simply time to manipulate art media, and is in direct contradiction to any comprehensive art education agenda.

As is true with all art experiences, educators play a vital role in children's art encounters. Cole and Schaefer (1990: 35) note that open dialogue about artworks starts when children begin to name their scribbles; the authors call the teacher '*the facilitator* . . . who guides the encounter between artwork and child'. Educators, as well as being the facilitators of the experience, also show children that art is much more than 'making something', that it is part of daily life, that it is accessible, and that, in art, they are active and important participators. Eisner aptly states:

> Let us be clear about the fact that the ability to experience the arts of our culture is not an automatic consequence of maturation. What children are able to think about, what they are able to experience, the distance their imaginative life allows them to travel, is shaped by the kind of educational lives they have had an opportunity to lead.
>
> (1985: 64)

As educators, we are responsible for offering children opportunities to participate in the art world – for creating an art world right there in the classroom. We must not forget, however, that the children we teach are in the foundation year, and that our aim is not to produce a group of very young art historians, but rather to establish in children an awareness, understanding, and appreciation of artworks, artists, and culture, as well as showing them the relevance of art in their everyday existence.

However, some educators suggest they do not feel knowledgeable enough to use cultural objects and/or artworks in their teaching. Many believe they are unequipped to provide children with worthwhile art encounters. Limited or, in many cases, no training in the area of art history and appreciation causes many educators to abandon the subject completely. As previously mentioned, our objective is not to deliver a dry chronicle of art's historical past, our aim is to show children their connection to art and provide them with relevant encounters with art. Every day, educators teach maths or science, does it follow that all educators are expert mathematicians or celebrated scientists? Some may be, but it is more probable that many have simply learned basic mathematical or scientific concepts successfully enough to share this knowledge with children. The same holds true for art, when educators let go of preconceived notions about art, become more acquainted with cultural and artistic objects, and see the connection art has to their own daily life, providing children with opportunities in art beyond mere fabrication activities will become second nature.

What are encounters with art?

There are many models we can implement to support an in-depth art programme. One already referred to called discipline-based art education or DBAE, was initiated in the early 1980s by the Getty Center for Education in the Arts. DBAE promotes art programmes that draw on the disciplines of art history, art criticism, art production, and aesthetics. In DBAE, the four disciplines make up a holistic art experience. A report by the Getty Center for Education in the Arts (1985: 13) states: 'The information derived from each of these disciplines and their interrelationships contributes significantly to a fuller and richer understanding of art.' Proponents of DBAE assert they do not support or follow one standard curriculum, but that the DBAE ideology should be adapted to the requirements of the educational establishment. Furthermore, supporters emphasise that each discipline is not taught as a separate subject, but rather that all four disciplines contribute to artistic experiences in an interrelated and connected fashion (Getty 1985; Herberholz and Hanson 1995).

The basic ideas that comprise DBAE, for example, that both looking at and creating art offer insight into the human condition and facilitate the communication of cultural principles (Getty 1985), are very similar to the ideas that underpin our comprehensive early years art education model. However, both in spite of this similarity and connection, and the fact that DBAE is accepted in many primary schools, we follow Schiller (1995) and question its practice in an early years setting. Is a programme that incorporates art history, art criticism, aesthetics, and art production too advanced for the Foundation Stage? After direct observation of her own practice along with a review of the literature, Schiller (1995: 38) concluded that 'there are activities in a developmentally appropriate curriculum that can take art activities to another level, one of discussion and understanding'.

Before going any further, with the ideas of DBAE fresh in our minds, we look at our own working definition of *encountering art* in the early years.

Definition of encountering art experiences

Our description of encountering art is based loosely on the underlying principles of DBAE and geared to the developmental capabilities of the early years. It includes looking at, discussing, reflecting upon, judging, understanding, and ultimately growing from art's past, present, and future, transmission of the world's diverse cultural values, crafts, folk art, artefacts, and learning about artists and artisans, museums and galleries, and art in everyday life such as functional art, television, fashion, and design. The aim here is to include in our definition of encountering art all the elements that contribute to the rich and complex world of art. Note, although a separate section, later in this chapter, is included to clarify the definition of 'multicultural art', all of the following information is applied to experiences with art and craft from both, so-called, Western and non-Western cultures.

What are some typical encounters with art based on the given definition? Provided encounters are developmentally on target, experiences can range from responding and discussing works of art by modern masters to becoming one of the expressive clouds in a Van Gogh painting. Children can visit an artist's studio, have a craftsperson come to the class, or take a trip to a museum. We encounter art when we dress up in the typical fashion of people from a foreign destination, when we study the carving of an African mask, make a fresco inspired by the Sistine Chapel, or when we pretend to be a Navajo weaver in America's southwest. The list of experiences is quite endless; however, before looking any further, it is important to address the developmental capabilities and aesthetic preferences of children encountering art. A brief summary in this area enables us to create and facilitate appropriate and meaningful experiences that start with a thorough knowledge of the learner.

Young children's cognitive capabilities and aesthetic preferences

Kerlavage (1995) points out that many researchers have tried to determine whether children, in their encounters and subsequent reflection and understanding of works of art, move through a succession of stages, similar to those established in artistic development. After an extensive review of the literature, Kerlavage (ibid.: 58) concluded, 'Children in the early childhood years travel through three progressive and sequential stages.' Encompassed in these stages are the changes in children's responses to artworks, including personal likes and dislikes, and the subsequent justification of the admired or objectionable work; children's articulation of the justifications and reflections; and their thoughts about art. Kerlavage (ibid.) identifies the three stages as 'sensorial, concrete, and expressive', and believes most early years children to be in the sensorial stage.

From both Kerlavage's (1995) discussion and summary of the literature, and direct observation we recognise that children in the *sensorial stage* learn about and encounter art through the senses, they are inclined to prefer artworks that elicit a pleasant sensory response, are drawn to beautiful vibrant colour, enjoy pattern, and are sometimes influenced by what the work aims to depict. Children appear to prefer artworks and subjects they can identify with, and take pleasure in works with a bold abstract nature. We have already established children in this stage are quite capable of discussing, looking at, and learning from encounters with art; however, Kerlavage (ibid.: 60) makes clear, children's experiences with art 'need to be considered from the standpoint of total sensory involvement'. In other words, when encountering art, always encourage children to actively use their senses; facilitate learning through touch, acting, pretending, and doing. Keep in mind similar to the stages of artistic development described in Chapter 1, though knowledge of the classic features of the sensorial stage offers us insight into the aesthetic preferences and cognitive capabilities of the early years child, they are not to be thought of as limitations, but as starting points, the base we build upon. In view of the fact that most children in the early years are in the sensorial stage described above and that early childhood is our focus, details regarding both the *concrete* and *expressive* stage are only touched upon. For more information on the stages, see Kerlavage (1995).

As children mature and establish their own complex symbol system, they enter the *concrete* stage. This stage is marked by less of an inclination to rely on sensory response and more of a tendency to rely on concrete evidence displayed in the work. Finally, children move into the *expressive* stage, a stage characterised by thinking in the abstract. Children in this group are able to participate in interpretative, aesthetic, and analytic discussions about works of art (Kerlavage 1995).

Encountering art objectives

Before describing how and when to encounter art, we look at some of the educational objectives we wish to achieve in such encounters. Defining our intentions helps guide and gives meaning to our experiences. Listed below is a collection of general objectives. The idea is to look at, add to, and use these objectives as potential headings under which to generate encountering art experiences. Readers will wish to add their own objectives based on any number of variables:

• To cultivate an understanding and appreciation of the practice, art, artefacts, and artistic traditions of diverse world cultures – this includes the child's own individual cultural heritage.
• To establish the active desire to look at, understand, and respond to works of fine art from people of both genders, of all cultures, from all parts of the world – including paintings, prints, sculpture, drawing among other two- and three-dimensional forms.

- To instigate the admiration and understanding of craft, functional art, folk art, artefacts, art used in rituals, holidays, and in daily life. To learn that art forms stretch beyond traditional fine arts and include movies, photographs, fashion, architecture, and various everyday objects.
- Understand what an artist or craftsperson is, where they work, what they do, their important and integral role in the formation of their particular culture.
- Learn about the places that house art, craft, and artefacts – museums, galleries, schools, places of religious worship, and the like.
- To see the connection between their own artistic endeavours and the endeavours of both those in the past and present; to recognise themselves as participators in culture.
- To build up a vocabulary of artistic terminology; to use descriptive and artistic terminology when discussing works of art.
- To learn how to 'read' visual imagery, to interpret, analyse, describe, and ultimately judge it.
- To make art part of everyday living, to learn through it, to build an awareness of it, and to see its influence not only in the 'adult world', but in the child's individual world; to see themselves actively involved in the art world.

While almost every encounter with art will be based on one or more of these objectives, educators need to include a number of specific objectives depending on the nature of the experience. For example, a trip to the museum based on the broad objective – learning about the places that house art, craft, and artefacts – must be guided by objectives that are more specific, created specially around the context in which the visit is taking place. For instance, if children are visiting the museum to look at Greek pottery, a more precise aim might include learning about the uses of Greek pots in everyday Greek life.

The how and when of art encounters

This next section explores how to talk to children about art and when to encounter art in the classroom.

How to talk to children about works of art

Without training in art education, it is difficult for educators to know how they should talk to children about artworks. Research on the subject turns up a variety of methods one can employ when discussing works of art with children (Chapman 1978; Cole and Schaefer 1990; Feeney and Moravcik 1987; Gilliatt 1983; Herberholz and Hanson 1995). However, among all of the literature there emerges one model that appears to serve as the framework around which numerous approaches are built. This method involves four parts: *description, analysis, interpretation*, and *judgement*. After a study involving over 450 children, Gilliatt (1983) concluded that this model is uncomplicated and easily employed by

Table 3.2 Art elements and principles

Art elements	Principles of art
Colour – wavelength of light reflected off an object. Primary colours include red, blue, and yellow. The secondary colours include orange, green, and purple. Hue identifies the colour, value refers to the lightness or darkness of a colour, and intensity refers to the brightness or dullness of a colour.	Unity – the arrangement of elements to create a sense of wholeness in the composition.

Variety and harmony – variety creates interest in a work of art by combining one or more of the art elements; harmony is the restful appearance a work will have, it is created when elements fit together well. |
| Form and shape – shape is an area enclosed by another art element such as line or colour; form is a shape that appears three-dimensional. | Emphasis – is created by highlighting an art element.

Rhythm and movement – rhythm is created by repeating an art element; movement gives a work of art the appearance of action, movement guides the eye through a work. |
| Line – the path of a continuous point through space; defines space, shape and forms, or can be implied by the edge of an object. | |
| Texture – surface of a work; texture can be physically felt or implied.

Space – areas around, between, above, below, and within things. | Balance – arrangement of elements in such a way that the work appears stable, no one section of the work seems heavier than any other part. |

educators regardless of their training. The following describes the four parts of the model that educators and children should move through when discussing objects and works of art:

1   *Description*: Begin a discussion about artwork or objects with description. Gilliatt (1983: 80–81) defines description as 'basically an inventory process in which the viewer examines what is immediately presented in the art object'. Children are asked to list everything they see in the object or work, including identifying the *art elements* or the building blocks of art (see Table 3.2). The art elements are regarded as the building blocks of art; these building blocks are tied together using the principles of art. Both the art elements and the principles of art are often termed the 'language of art'; think of the art elements as words and the principles of art as how we put those words together to form, first sentences, and then complete compositions. Gilliatt considers description the most vital step of the approach; the list that children compile in this stage influences the rest of the discussion. There are many ways to elicit this dialogue. Educators can make it into a game, similar to a treasure hunt, and ask the children to seek out all of the objects and art elements in the work, or educators can ask children to find their favourite colour within the object,

to look for interesting textures, to locate shapes. This stage should continue until everything is identified.

2   *Analysis*: Next, analyse the work. When we analyse a work of art we look at how the elements of art relate to both each other and to the artwork as a whole. In analysis, we discover and talk about the *principles of art* (see Table 3.2) or about how the art elements work together. The principles of art are unity, variety and harmony, emphasis, rhythm and movement, and balance. They are interdependent on one another, and in many works of art are difficult to single out. Because art is analysed using the principles of art, an understanding of them is important. Encourage children to respond to how colours look next to each other (unity, variety and harmony), ask children to find the biggest and smallest shapes (emphasis), involve children in a dialogue about lines that look the same, ask children where they see the similar lines, and count how many lines there are (rhythm).

3   *Interpretation*: After analysing the artwork or object, we interpret it. In fact, when we discuss mood, emotion, or how an object or painting makes us feel, we are taking part in art interpretation. During interpretation, educators aim to elicit a response based on the two earlier stages. For example, when looking at a portrait painting educators might ask children what they think the person in the portrait does for a living. Educators guide children to base their answer on clues from the former stages. They could ask the children to look again at the dress of the person, at the background, or search for other clues that could indicate the person's profession. Because the nature of interpretation is subjective, questioning will elicit a number of varying responses. Imagination and perception work together in interpretation.

4   *Judgement*: The last step is to judge the work. Judgement is usually considered the formal assessment of a work of art based on its respective artistic style. For example, in typical judgement, a work would first be labelled as 'realistic' or 'abstract' or categorised using any number of different classification systems, and then it would be judged as to whether or not it is representative of that style. However, in order to keep our dialogue developmentally accurate, Cole and Schaefer (1990: 37) suggest we instead ask children to make 'personal' judgements about the work based on the previous three stages. For example, we can ask children if they would like to buy the object or painting and why, or we could have children compare two paintings, ask them which one they prefer and encourage them to state their reasons for choosing one over the other (ibid.).

When talking about art, educators should aim to employ proper art terminology and encourage children to do the same.

Another important 'how' consideration

The model previously described is only a skeleton or frame; in order to make encounters with art meaningful, the experience needs to employ the children's natural way of learning within their given maturational level.

As previously indicated, children in the early years tend to learn about and respond to art through the senses. Therefore, to make art learning meaningful, all of the senses must be involved. To clarify, just as we emphasise use of the senses in both aesthetic and art making experiences, we must strive to do the same when children encounter art. The following are just a taste of the many ways to support multi-sensory learning in encountering art experiences.

- When looking at and discussing paintings, ask children what they think the flowers, inside of the house, the animal, the picnic smells, feels, tastes, or sounds like.
- When studying a sculpture, ask children to pick a spot on the sculpture they would sit, stand, or hide under if they were an ant. Encourage children to imagine themselves running around the outside of the sculpture, at what point would they fall off? Where would they get back on? Try to look at and experience original sculptures rather than pictures of them whenever possible.
- When learning about painting, printing, sculpture, ceramics, or crafts, interest children in the process or medium used. For example, before, during, or after looking at a weaving, ask children to create one for themselves.
- Look at textures in two-dimensional work and try to find the same textures in the natural and constructed environment.
- When discussing functional art, ask children to seek out a piece of functional art and use it in their own daily activity.
- Experience artefacts and ritual objects first-hand, for example, do not just look at pictures of masks, be inspired to create your own and use them in a pretend ritual. Alternatively, find an original mask, bring it to the classroom, and let children use it in play.

When to encounter art

Moving on from how to engage children in dialogue about art objects is the question of when we should partake in encounters with art. Again, we begin with knowledge of the child's natural tendencies for acquiring knowledge and making meaning. As reviewed, the DBAE approach, from which we form our definition of encountering art, does not teach each discipline (to reiterate, art history, art production, art criticism, and aesthetics) separately; rather the disciplines are taught in relation to each other forming a holistic art experience. We base our approach on the same idea, yet we teach holistically because the child's developmental needs warrant it. Kerlavage (1995: 60) states, 'Children process information in a holistic manner; therefore, teachers need to structure programs which enhance and increase children's knowledge and skill at making art, perceiving art, and reflecting on art rather than depending on formal discussion and analysis.'

How does this relate to when we should encounter art? Learning holistically implies that learning is most meaningful when experienced within the context of related, connected, or relevant experiences. Art, therefore, is best encountered, and perhaps most meaningful, within the context of children's daily experiences (Kerlavage 1995). For example, filling terracotta pots with soil for tiny seedlings could spark off a discussion about Mexican ceramics, or, in another example, children playing dress-up are easily guided into a discussion on anything from functional art to textiles to world cultures. While this may seem a simple concept, similar to the perceptual sensitivity demanded of educators with respect to initiating, seeking out and guiding aesthetic experiences, recognising these meaningful times to encounter art or, to borrow once again Schaefer and Cole's (1990) term, 'teachable moments' demands the educator have a guiding plan and time for keen observation.

Though we have established that art is best encountered in daily experience, we can not, in any way, assume that educators, especially those with little to no training in art, will know when to encounter art or how to make a natural connection between the child's experience and, say, the work of a contemporary artist. It is with this assumption that we take the basic premise of children's holistic learning and describe three suitable times to encounter art.

- *In the context of an art making experience*: Gardner (1989: 76) states, 'Perceptual, historical, critical, and other "peri-artistic" activities should be closely related to, and (whenever possible) emerge from, the child's pro-ductions.' This idea is echoed by Kolbe (1993: 79) who suggests acquainting children with artworks 'similar in spirit to the children's own work'. To introduce art in the context of an art making experience, educators need to be aware not only of the children's productions, but also of their processes. Connections are easily made that relate to the process they are using or the medium they employ. For instance, children learning about textiles would benefit greatly from a visit to see a working loom. On the other hand, a child who loves to paint large colourful shapes would be open to looking at and discussing the work of any number of abstract artists.
- *As motivation*: Encounter art as a stimulus to an art making experience. When using a work of art to inspire or motivate, use the model described earlier in this chapter (description, analysis, interpretation, and judgement), encourage children to talk not only about the work itself, but also about the processes and media the artist employed. Connect the encounter with the planned art making experience. Artworks and objects, used in motivation, are not shown and discussed so children can emulate them, they are shown to stimulate and excite children into taking off on their own artistic journey. Motivational matter

includes works of art, crafts, artefacts, museum and gallery visits, a visit to an artist's studio, a walk around a textile factory, or a stroll through the neighbourhood looking at the local architecture. For example, pretending to be in a Native American 'Rain Dance' is a wonderful use of encounters with art as the motivation to a subsequent production experience making Native American regalia. Refer to Chapter 2 for more on motivation, and to Figure 2.1 (Chapter 2) to see the connection between motivation and encounters with art.

- *In the context of learning new artistic techniques or concepts*: Encounter art when children appear ready and able to learn a new skill or concept. For example, if children seem ready to use scissors, introduce them to the work of collage artists, show them what is possible, and relate the work to both the process involved and their newly maturing skill. If children are learning a new concept, such as colours or shapes, educators can choose from any number of sources (for example, artists, artefacts, functional art) to reinforce learning and stimulate further interest in the concept.

Although the times described offer educators a chance to construct a prescribed plan for encounters with art, learning more about art and culture will enable staff to introduce art encounters with greater ease, and at times, perhaps unplanned, throughout the course of the day. Finally, as educators themselves start to learn more about art, and continue supporting encounters at the planned times, they should also aim to make art an integral part of the children's daily experience. For example, initiate art games that involve matching, sorting, and comparing art reproduction flashcards. Bring art into the classroom, enable children to use and connect with art by talking about and making available colourful books and objects of functional art. Invite an artist or craftsperson into the class for a demonstration or discussion. Acquaint children with art concepts and cultural and artistic objects using an in-class gallery or, if space is an issue, set up a bulletin board featuring an artist, culture, or theme of the week. Note, when displaying reproductions and other works of art, educators should think about both the work they display and how long they display it for. Gilliatt (1983) argues that if the same work stays up for too long, it will lose its initial impact; consequently, interest in looking at the work wanes and ultimately disappears. Change work frequently, but ensure success by allowing ample time for children to know, study, and live with a particular artwork. Strive to bring the world of art directly into the children's lives.

Multicultural art

In our definition of encountering art, children are introduced to artwork, artefacts, craft, folk art, and other traditional and fine art objects from diverse cultures and peoples throughout the world. Moreover, the children not only examine the physical outpourings of these sources, but also learn about cultural traditions and the lives of the artists and craftspeople within those diverse cultures. Because of the enormous breadth of this definition, the inclusion of a lengthy discourse on multicultural art is superfluous. What is more, it is quite hard to conjure up images of an educational art programme that does not draw inspiration from artists and cultures of all race and gender. An arts education curriculum that promotes only the work of, for instance, twentieth-century European males (think Pablo Picasso or Salvador Dali), would not be considered sound or, for that matter, accurate in today's definition of an inclusive arts programme. However, as the term multicultural art is used so often and because its ideology plays such a fundamental part in any in-depth and complete art curriculum, it is important educators are familiar with its meaning.

A basic definition of multicultural art is the study of the artistic and aesthetic endeavours of the people and cultures that form the non-Western world. Delacruz (1995: 102) adds that a multicultural arts curriculum should also include reflection upon and equal exposure to the work of 'minority groups, and women and reflect the significance of folk art, the crafts, mass-produced objects, and mass-circulated images'. However, as Delacruz illustrates, there is more to a multicultural arts education than simply looking at and acknowledging the work of diverse cultures; there is the transmission of cultural values, the communication and exploration of the human experience, and the integral role the artist and craftsperson play in cultural identity:

> In a multicultural art curriculum the art, artefacts, crafts, ritual, and domestic objects fashioned by generations of artisans become the subjects of interest that inform and expand children's frames of reference. The subject of interest is not limited, however, to formal and technical accomplishments, but includes meaning, symbolism, intention, function, and both relative and universal values. The subject is the artist, the culture, the purposeful processes and products of human concern.
>
> (ibid.: 103)

Comparing the description of multicultural art with the definition of encountering art experiences presented in this book, it is apparent that although we aim to include in our discussions works and objects chosen under the principles of cultural and gender equality, we need to be mindful of the way we teach it. Merely showing children works by various groups of people from around the world is not enough. Multiculturalism demands we examine the artistic traditions and artisans within both the context of the particular culture and within the scope of the human experience. In other words, educators, whenever possible, should move beyond looking and discussing art and attempt to expose relationships and links between the object, the maker, and the universal human experience (ibid.). Questions that stretch past description, analysis, interpretation, and judgement and address more universal feelings, emotions, desires, and concerns such as love, hate, or perhaps survival, aid in highlighting this connection. Remaining conscious of this point and engaging in encounters with art, based on our far-reaching definition, educators can be certain they are effectively participating and engaging in multicultural art experiences.

See Appendix 2 for further resources on encounters with art.

Chapter 4

Documentation and special needs:

Reaching *all* children, and documenting it as we go along

The first part of this chapter looks at the recording of artistic experience, examines the role of assessment in art in early childhood, and offers educators guidelines for successful documentation. The second part of this chapter is given over to an examination of teaching art to children with special needs. In observance and subsequent implementation of the statutory inclusion of special needs children in the classroom or nursery, a look at the methodology for teaching art to special needs is required.

DOCUMENTATION OF THE EXPERIENCE

What is documentation?

Documentation is the constant recording, revisiting, reflection, and interpretation of pertinent comments, dialogue, actions, visual work, and observations of children and educators taken throughout artistic experiences. Figure 4.1 illustrates an example of basic documentation. Recognise, though documentation is exemplified as happening before, during, and after an art experience, in practice it is similar to motivation and dialogue in that it is continuous. Think of documentation as an uninterrupted cycle. At the start of an experience, educators record children's comments and actions: this guides the experience and reveals children's interests; and refer to past documentation: the revisiting of past documentation enables children to see links in their experiences, and provides material that may serve as a starting point for the next adventure. Documentation continues into the hands-on experience itself. The educator's documentation of children's comments, actions, discoveries, and visual work gives staff and children the opportunity to see the process unfold; furthermore, this documentation enables educators and children to make connections, dream up future experiences, and take control of their learning. After the heart of an experience, documentation of the children's visual work, comments, and actions opens up reflection upon the process and serves as the foundation on which to build the next experience. Similar to documentations use at the start of the experience, documentation at the end fuels the next

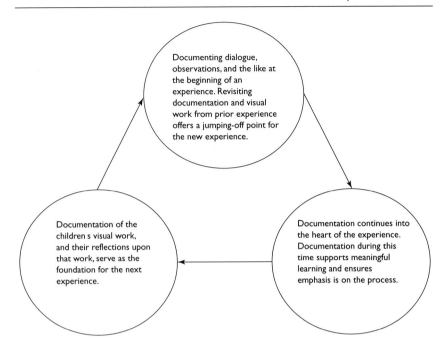

Figure 4.1 Basic documentation

exploration. All documentation must be revisited throughout the experience for this cycle to take place.

Continuous documentation, another integral element in our holistic model, helps drive, tie together, and link the components of artistic experience including encounters with art, art making, and aesthetic experiences. This relationship is illustrated in Figure 4.2. Educators use documentation, together with motivation and dialogue, to propel artistic experience, extend and ensure experiences lead to further endeavours, link the forms of art experience, and support relevant and meaningful art endeavours. For example, imagine children are encountering art by looking at and discussing cave paintings, and a dialogue ensues about the shapes used to represent animals. Educators recording pertinent comments jot down the children's interest in the unusual shapes, and later, after revisiting the documentation, might decide the children's interest points to an art making experience, in this instance, possibly creating imaginary 'shape' animals out of clay. This art making experience is documented and reflection upon that documentation will inevitably lead to further experiences. See Figure 4.3 for another example of how documentation links, extends, and supports meaningful art experiences.

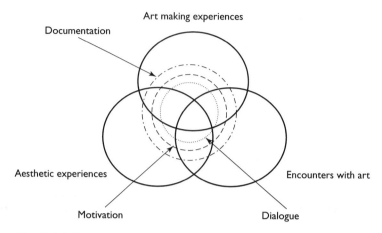

Figure 4.2 Model of art programme with documentation. Documentation is an important and necessary element in our holistic model

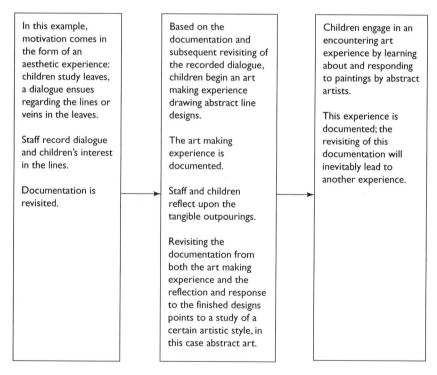

In this example, motivation comes in the form of an aesthetic experience: children study leaves, a dialogue ensues regarding the lines or veins in the leaves.

Staff record dialogue and children's interest in the lines.

Documentation is revisited.

Based on the documentation and subsequent revisiting of the recorded dialogue, children begin an art making experience drawing abstract line designs.

The art making experience is documented.

Staff and children reflect upon the tangible outpourings.

Revisiting the documentation from both the art making experience and the reflection and response to the finished designs points to a study of a certain artistic style, in this case abstract art.

Children engage in an encountering art experience by learning about and responding to paintings by abstract artists.

This experience is documented; the revisiting of this documentation will inevitably lead to another experience.

Figure 4.3 Documentation in practice

Actively implemented documentation also serves to support:

- the creation of a curriculum based on the needs and desires of the child;
- insight into, among other things, a child's learning style, maturational level, and artistic processes. This insight enables staff to define teaching strategies based on how the children learn and what the children want to learn, rather than on what we, as adults, think we should teach them.
- flexible and adaptable experiences;
- communication with parents, staff, and the community;
- an opportunity for the children to look at and build on their own experiences and the experiences of others;
- the building of children's confidence; children see the control they have over their own learning, and the importance of their participation in group discussions;
- staff reflection on their own teaching practice;
- correct intervention into children's artistic endeavours.

Finally, documentation is essential to assessment; accurate assessment is fully reliant on thorough documentation practices. This being the case, before learning more about documentation, we briefly turn our attention to assessment, an incredibly important area of early childhood education.

Assessment

When we assess, we evaluate the quality or nature of something. In the case of art in the early years, when we assess we look at the experience, the child, how the child changes because of the experience, and the processes the child uses within the experience. Despite the fact that assessment plays a major role in general education, Wright (1994) points out that many view assessment as the antithesis of early childhood art. Some educators feel there is nothing to assess, that it is too hard to quantify growth or learning in art, that expression or creativity is too difficult to measure. Others believe assessment automatically indicates the judgement of finished artworks, and feel the very idea of such a practice is in direct contrast with an early years focus on the process.

With the introduction of the early learning goals, and growing popularity of DBAE, such beliefs are becoming outdated; objectives associated with a more educational and focused art curriculum rely on assessment. A review of the literature supports the notion that if we want to promote, facilitate, and be part of the artistic endeavours of children, assessment is crucial. What is more, a disregard of assessment in art points to a disregard of the subject as both important to a child's development and as a discipline worthy of study (Barnes 1987; Eisner 1972, 1988; Gardner 1988; Wright 1994). Eisner (1988: 7) states, 'To the extent that arts are neglected in assessment program, they will be neglected in other ways also.'

While those opposed to assessment believe that art learning is too difficult to measure, research indicates otherwise. The literature reveals that there are many areas in early childhood art that can be easily assessed and evaluated, that are quantifiable or measurable (Barnes 1987; Eisner 1972; Gardner 1988; Herberholz and Hanson 1995; Wright 1994). Some of these areas include:

- perceptual, aesthetic, and cognitive development;
- technical skills and use of materials;
- expressive and artistic development;
- social and personal development.

For a more specific assessment list, see Table 4.1.

Educators should not only assess the children's development, but must also assess and evaluate the following:

- art materials;
- the physical learning environment;
- the social and emotional learning environment;
- the curriculum;
- the educators' teaching practices.

Table 4.1 Measurable areas in art assessment

Perceptual, aesthetic, and cognitive development
Engages in discovery and investigation
Notices details
Exercises perceptual discrimination
Builds on prior information
Uses the senses to extract information from the environment
Uses the senses to extract information from works of art
Reflects on own works of art
Reflects on own artistic processes
Sees connections in artistic experiences
Connects encounters with art to own art making experiences
Sees similarities and differences in objects and works of art
Sees similarities and differences in objects
Understands nature's role as provider of media and inspiration
Develops and decodes simple symbols

Table 4.1 continued

Perceptual, aesthetic, and cognitive development

Technical skill and use of art media

Uses two-dimensional media with purpose

Uses three-dimensional media with purpose

Can handle a selection of drawing tools with dexterity

Can handle a selection of painting media with dexterity

Understands and uses natural objects as art media

Chooses suitable media to task at hand

Consistently developing new skills and techniques

Is inventive with art media

Builds on previously learned skills and techniques

Expressive and artistic development

Is able to give form to expression

Overcomes obstacles in the giving of form to expression

Demonstrates progression through stages of artistic development

Understands art as a way to express thoughts and ideas

Uses creative thinking in the giving of form to expression

Is inventive in expression

Uses art as a mode of communication

Social and personal development

Engages in dialogue about art with other children and staff

Treats own art, art of others, art reproductions, and objects with care

Takes turn leading projects and allowing others to lead

Cares for art media, natural objects, and natural and constructed environment

Knowing what we should be looking at, the question remains, how do we carry out assessment in early childhood art? Wright points out, assessment, in early years art, is not accomplished through standardised tests or cold objective measuring instruments, instead assessment is accomplished through sensitive 'observation' and the subsequent reflection and 'interpretation' of what is noted.

> observation and interpretation of children's involvement in the arts enable the early childhood teacher to guide children's learning in the arts. While informal observations have generally been used to assist teachers' program planning and evaluation, they can also be used for informal assessment of children's arts experiences in relation to program continuity. Qualitative, observation-based assessment also provides a means with which to provide feedback to children, parents, and educational administrators about individual and group achievements.
>
> (1994: 28)

Observation-based assessment happens throughout the course of an experience. The documentation taken during observations, which, in turn, provides the information used for making sound assessments, involves much more than ticking off of items on a list. The documentation for observation-based assessment must be in-depth, thorough, and continuous. Observations are documented throughout the course of experiences, revisited, and interpreted on a constant basis. In observation-based assessment, educators study the information collected through various methods (outlined later in this section) and apply any significant findings to the different areas we have named as quantifiable in early years art (ibid.). Refer to Figure 4.1 for those areas.

Note all information hereafter applies to documentation used in both art assessment and artistic experiences.

What do we document?

With a better understanding of what documentation is and what purpose it serves, we go on to look at the material we document. This includes three items:

- observations;
- dialogue;
- visual work (visual work we have established as the visual outpourings of experience).

Through the collection of observations, dialogue, and visual work educators should seek to uncover, and be on the lookout for the following:

- a child's developmental level;
- what children are interested in learning;

- ideas for future experiences;
- individual learning styles (the way in which a child learns best – through vision, touch, and so forth);
- readiness for skill acquisition;
- children's frustrations or boredom with a media;
- children's success with materials.

Use observations, dialogue, and visual work to do the following:

- study the children;
- create a relevant and meaningful arts curriculum;
- know when to intervene and guide learning;
- provide positive constructive feedback and enter into necessary dialogue;
- show children connections between experiences;
- document children's processes;
- watch children's interactions with other children;
- teach skills with relevance;
- enrich and extend experiences;
- capitalise on the strengths of the child.

Observation

Documentation, in both assessment and in children's artistic experiences, depends on insightful observation. Educators should observe:

- *How a child uses art media*: Watch how children use media. Do they hold the brush properly? Does their handling of media hinder expression? Are they ready to learn a new skill? Does an old skill need to be re-taught? Can we extend learning by introducing a new material?
- *How a child turns expression into form*: Observe how children express themselves. How do they use the media? Do they articulate their expressions in dialogue? Do they rely on visual form to communicate their expression? How do they seem to feel after expressing in visual form? Do children seem satisfied with their work?
- *What a child plays with*: Watch what materials and toys children play with. Relate their choices to their art experiences. For example, if they always play with rectangular blocks, try introducing them to geometric shapes; absorb them in more construction activities, or think of other ways to connect their play with art experiences.
- *How a child plays*: Observe the child at play. Does the child take part mainly in hands-on activities? Pretend or role play experiences? Use a child's natural play type in their art experiences. If a child partakes mainly in playing dress-up, think of activities involving textiles, clothing from around the world, or talk about patterns and textures.

- *What children are drawn to, what inspires them, what do they talk about the most?* Be alert to what moves a child. What does the child choose to wear? Eat? What is the child's favourite animal? Movie? Also, be sensitive to what children do not say. Watch what area of the room they usually go to; look at their artworks, what do their visual outpourings tell you? What are they interested in?

Dialogue

Dialogue will form a large part of the information collected in documentation. Educators should listen for:

- *Dialogue between children*: Listen and document as children talk to each other during artistic experiences, in play, and during group discussions. What do they talk about? Do children seem to be interested in the project? Are they making connections? Is the experience relevant to their lives?
- *Dialogue between a child and a staff member*: Record not only your own conversations with children, but also dialogue between other staff and children. Are conversations similar? Is information revealed in your dialogue with the child similar or different to the information revealed when that same child speaks to other members of staff?
- *Dialogue a child has with her or himself during an experience*: Listen to what the child says during the process. Many times this kind of 'child-speak' is directive, informative, and can offer clues to the artistic processes of the child (Thompson and Bales 1991).
- *Dialogue within the group*: Listen for important comments children make during group discussions. Do the comments connect experiences? Demonstrate frustrations with art learning? Show growth or development?
- *Dialogue during artistic experience*: During all forms of art experience, listen for comments that help identify needs, frustrations, the process the child is using; take note of dialogue that can be used to connect learning areas or extend the experience.
- *Dialogue during reflection upon visual work*: Comments made during reflection upon visual work can expose frustrations with a process used, reveal blossoming interests, or can be used to extend an experience.
- *Pertinent comments*: During all types of dialogue listen for comments that can be used to extend learning, lead to a new experience, display misconceptions, or demonstrate frustration. Remind children of these comments, show them what they said, and use their comments to guide teaching practice, and capitalise on the children's strengths.

For more information on dialogue, see Chapter 2.

Visual work

The tangible nature of visual work makes it an incredible form of documentation. Collect finished products as well as casual scribbles, mark making, doodles, and exercises with media. Also look at work in progress and collect photographs of temporary work such as block constructions or forms created in the sand-pit. In documentation, visual work serves various functions.

- *Extends or leads to new experiences*: A close look at the visual work collected for documentation supports the extension of an experience or can point to new connected experiences. Notice the processes, concepts, media used, and apply these features to extended or new, but relevant endeavours.
- *Reveals needed skills*: Reflection on children's visual work documents and demonstrates skill proficiency or deficiency, and concretely shows educators what skills children need to learn, re-learn, or practise.
- *Is a map of the process*: We learned that visual work is the tangible remnant of the process. Examining visual work helps us see where the process took us, how the process changed us, how we changed the process.

Methods of documentation

We have discovered that observations, dialogue, and children's visual works provide us with the material to be gathered, but what methods do we employ to collect all of this information? First, educators should be aware that, in practice, documentation is rather complex and can sometimes prove time-consuming. When implementing parts of the Reggio Emilia principles into their own programme Kantor and Whaley write:

> We 'heard' our Italian mentors tell us that documentation is key; but, admittedly, it was the last piece we explored as we tried ideas in our own classroom. It was the most difficult piece to incorporate into our day. Even the mechanical aspects of keeping a camera and tape recorder available seemed overwhelming at first, but our motivation increased once we realized how much insight we gained from listening to children's words and reviewing our notes. Documentation allows the teacher to be careful and effective while intervening.
>
> (1998: 323)

With this in mind, it is very important that educators make documentation as simple as possible. Thankfully, there are a number of easy ways to gather accurate documentation; three methods we explore here are: written documentation, photographic and multi-media documentation, and portfolios.

Written documentation

Observations and dialogue that take place throughout the course of the day can be written down in a notebook (designated for such a purpose) or on ready-made documentation sheets (see Figure 4.4). Have one educator document as the others involve children in dialogue. Scatter notebooks and writing instruments around the room for easy access, and have ready-made photocopies handy for jotting down quick notes. Use these materials when children's actions or comments could potentially enlighten staff or children, enrich the experience, support their learning, or generate further endeavours.

A few important points to remember when recording:

- Written documentation can take the form of brief notes, short anecdotes, or long narratives.
- Write neatly and coherently; staff will use and learn from each other's notes.
- Always write the context in which a comment was made or an action carried out (Thompson and Bales 1991); the interpretation of documentation relies on this (Wright 1994).
- Documentation is useless if it is not revisited. Strive to find time in the day to refer to, with both staff and children depending on the nature of the material, what has been learned, uncovered, or accomplished.

Photographic and multi-media documentation

Complete documentation goes beyond written recordings. Photographs of the children absorbed in all forms of artistic experiences, audiotapes of dialogue when working with staff, other children, or alone, and video footage of experiences are indispensable documentation tools. Rinaldi (1998: 120) comments on the Reggio Emilia's methods of documentation: 'We use written notes, observation charts, diaries, and other narrative forms, as well as audiotapes, photographs, slides, and videotapes. These allow us to make visible the process of children's learning.'

Photographs and slides of children's experiences and of their visual work open up communication with parents and remind children of their learning. The author's own practice reveals the use of audiotapes as the easiest and most thorough form of documentation. Brittain (1979) discovered a recording device placed near the easel captured information in a most non-threatening way. It can almost be guaranteed that throughout the course of the day milestones will be met, hurdles will be jumped, or discoveries will be made that staff will not be there to witness; having other methods of documentation available beside written observations and dialogue can minimise the risk of missing such monumental occasions.

Child's name and age: _____   **Date recorded:** _____

Name of documenter: _____   **Date revisited:** _____

Learning situation:

What was said by child or staff; what was observed by staff (tick off as necessary):

Notes and comments: future experiences, skills to be learned or practised, new objectives to be introduced, early learning goals, other (tick off as necessary):

Figure 4.4 Sample ready-made documentation sheet

Portfolios

Using a portfolio in documentation does not merely mean the collection of a few finished products stored away in a folder. Rather, a portfolio that contains a child's visual work, comments, recordings, photographs, and videos of various experiences. A portfolio only containing finished products will tell us nothing of the child's process. Just as written comments, observations, and photographs are interpreted and revisited, so we must revisit portfolios.

Writing about Arts PROPEL, an art education programme based on perception, reflection, as well as production, Gardner (1990: 46) describes student portfolios as 'process-folios'. In these process-folios Arts PROPEL students keep, among other items, rough drafts, written ideas, works by other artists, as well as their own finished pieces. Though Gardner is referring to an older student, the idea of trying to encapsulate the child's total art education experience in a portfolio echoes our own ideas about documentation.

To build, learn, and grow from portfolios; to designate portfolios as a form of documentation educators should include in them:

- paintings, drawings, and other visual works that demonstrate cognitive, perceptual, and aesthetic growth or change;
- significant dialogue pertaining to all forms of artistic experiences;
- video and audiotapes of dialogue and experiences;
- photographs of finished works, works in progress, temporary work, and photos of the child participating in all types of art experiences (including encounters with art and aesthetic experiences).

In short, keep in the portfolio all information that illustrates the child's processes, makes learning tangible, or can serve to enhance or connect future experiences.

Finally, a child's portfolio is meaningless unless we actively look at, learn from, revisit, and interpret its contents. In addition, portfolios are not only for staff to study, portfolios are an excellent tool for opening up communication with parents, and are an invaluable resource for children to reflect upon and see the path of their artistic learning.

Always remember, in all types of documentation, educators must refer to the information gathered and use that information to extend an experience, make learning more meaningful, ensure tasks are developmentally appropriate, inform teaching practice, begin new connected experiences, aid assessment, and so forth. There is no use collecting information if we are not going to use it. Documentation can only fulfil its educational potential if it is actively employed.

Before ending this section, we look at the display of children's art. Displays are a type of documentation, proof of experience, and have the potential to ignite further experience.

Displays

Similar to and simultaneously as a form of documentation, displays serve a variety of purposes including:

- advancing, enriching, and/or furthering artistic endeavours;
- defining the aesthetic character of the educational environment;
- fostering in children a respect for the constructed environment;
- exemplifying respect for the artistic process and subsequent visual forms;
- building on a child's sense of self-confidence and accomplishment;
- opening up communication and dialogue with parents and other outside members of the community.

Displays, like portfolios, are not created simply to summarise an experience. Displays are there to learn from, to extend learning, and facilitate communication. A display with this type of educational potential includes:

- the visual work of each child participating in the experience;
- both finished products and some works in progress;
- photographs of aesthetic, art making, and encounters with art experiences participated in during the course of the endeavour;
- written commentary of the processes involved, skills developed, and knowledge gained throughout the experience;
- details of children's significant comments, actions, or interactions that may have occurred during the experience.

Of course, there will be displays in the environment that will not be so comprehensive. For example, educators may choose to have a display of photographs illustrating an aesthetic experience children participated in, or a display might only feature some textures discovered on a nature walk. Regardless of the purpose, there are some basic guiding principles behind the creation of a display.

Content and intent

Before creating a display, educators need to ask themselves two questions. First, what is the content, the material, you want to display? Paintings? Sculpture? Photographs? The content you choose to display will affect how and where you are able to display the work. Second, educators should ask, why are we displaying this content? What is our intention? Is it for developmental purposes? Is it to be touched? Are we creating this display for the parents? The content and the intent will affect the entire display.

Location

Location depends on the content and intent of the display. For example, displays intended to be touched and explored by children should be hung in a place where children can easily engage in such action. On the other hand, displays of, say, three-dimensional fragile work, only meant to be looked at, would be better off displayed in, perhaps, a see-through enclosed space such as a showcase. Remember, displays need not only be created in the classroom; educators should use the entire learning centre and seek out locations in the community to display evidence of the children's artistic pursuits.

Labelling

For displays to teach, enrich, and extend learning, they need to be clearly labelled. Include the children's names, essential information regarding involved processes, and/or, depending on the intention, include individual narratives and significant commentary.

Lighting, colour, and mounts

Just as we would put care and thought into a display of adult work, we must do the same with children's art. Unfortunately, observation has demonstrated that many early childhood educators think children's visual work needs to be dressed up with frilly boarders, multi-coloured mounts, hung on strange angles, and lighting is usually forgotten about all together. The truth is children's art is strong enough to stand on its own. Children's art is best viewed in plenty of light, against a background colour that enhances and does not compete with the art. It should always be hung (or with three-dimensional work placed on a table) in a uniform fashion. Would we hang a painting in our living space on an angle? Most of us would not, first it would prove difficult to enjoy the work, and, second, it demonstrates disrespect for the art itself. Respect children's art, before hanging it up or arranging it on a table ask yourself, if this was a painting I made, how would I want it displayed?

Displays, similar to other forms of documentation, need to be revisited, talked about, and referred to if we wish them to fulfil their educational potential. Be sure to talk parents and other staff through new displays, encourage children to look back over their processes, to build on them, to think about what they learned, and to link the displayed experience with their present endeavour. Ask children to get involved in the making of a display; make the fabrication of a display an art experience. Finally, use displays to make every inch of the learning environment aesthetic, significant, stimulating, and inspiring.

SPECIAL NEEDS

Thus far, we have considered art experiences based on more or less a 'prescribed' model of artistic and aesthetic development; however, are we to assume that all children will naturally follow a typical developmental or physical path? Statistics from the Annual Schools' Census 2002 indicate that the number of school-age pupils in England with statements of Special Educational Needs (SEN) is approximately 3 per cent. Mindful of this number, and of the statutory *inclusion* policy, it is imperative educators know how to reach and support creative and artistic growth in *all* children.

Inclusion refers to the incorporation of children with special needs into the 'regular' educational setting; the goal of inclusion is to provide equal educational opportunities to all children regardless of disability or impediments. In early years centres across the country, children with developmental, physical, or emotional challenges work alongside children without those challenges everyday. With an inclusion policy already in place how can we ensure that each child in our care has an equal opportunity not to only participate in artistic experiences, but also to develop and learn because of those experiences?

Fortunately, art is easily adaptable to both typical and challenged children; furthermore, many of the special needs approaches or adaptations educators would use in, say, a year five setting are already implemented as standard practice in early years art. For instance, early childhood art's focus on the process is advocated at all educational levels in the teaching of art to special needs (Anderson 1994; Henley 1992). Regardless of any overlap the reader may notice, our goal is to achieve success in our educational practices and in the children's experiences. In order to do so there are a number of approaches and guidelines educators can implement.

Approaches and guidelines for special needs

Individualised attention

Individualised attention does not simply mean spending time with children when they are painting alone at an easel. True individualised attention, especially that associated with special needs, starts with a thorough knowledge of the child's developmental or physical challenge. Special needs as a category cover a very broad spectrum of challenges. After reviewing the literature (Anderson 1994; Henley 1992; Papalia and Olds 1993), they are referred to in four broad categories: physically challenged, developmentally or cognitively challenged, emotionally challenged, and, we add this fourth classification, the artistically gifted.

Individualised attention demands the educator have knowledge of a given child's special need, strengths and weaknesses, how far along a child is in learning certain skills, understands what motivates the child, and as a result of this knowledge is more able to support that child's artistic and aesthetic development (Henley

1992). This knowledge is gleaned through a number of activities such as dialogue with the child during art experiences, listening to a child's reflection on the process, and through insightful observation and documentation. Additionally, maintaining a balance in the classroom between an individualised, small group, and large group instruction will ensure children get to spend some time, during the course of the day, engaged in a one-on-one interaction with a member of staff.

Normalise the experience

We normalise the art experience when we 'choose and adopt media and themes which put children on equal footing' (Henley 1992: 23). Henley refers to normalising the experience as 'camouflaging', and he notes that by camouflaging our goal is not to forget about a child's special need, but rather to '*camouflage a child's weaknesses and exploit whatever strengths he or she possesses*'. By normalising the art experience, we encourage and support artistic learning and development in all children. There are many ways to normalise the experience. One way is through adaptation of media, technique, and theme.

Adaptation

To properly support children in their artistic experiences educators will have to make certain adjustments in any number of areas including, but not limited to, materials, teaching methods, chosen theme or content, motivation, skills and techniques, and the actual art making environment. Adaptations are based on the child's individual needs, the type of special need, and the nature of the media, theme, or technique. It is important to note, that adaptations should be made with the principle of normalisation or camouflaging in mind. In other words, adaptations are not there to call attention to the child's need; instead, they offer children a chance to have the same opportunity for art experiences as every other child in the class.

As indicated, adaptations rely on, among other variables, the nature of both the child's special need and the media or technique used. For example, a child with visual impairments will need media adapted in a much different way than a child with emotional disturbances. In another example, adaptations for painting are quite different from adaptations applied in construction or ceramics. Adaptations come in many forms and could include larger handles on brushes, dripless paint, Braille signage, or special scissors. Other types of adaptations include offering pre-cut shapes to a child who is unable to use scissors or using glue sticks instead of school glue.

In the early years, as fingers are small, muscles are still growing, and techniques are quite basic, adaptations for children with special needs are minimal. Unless the child has acute physical impairments, educators should try to exercise restraint in offering too many adaptations. This brings us to the next principle – maintaining the least restrictive environment.

Least restrictive environment

Part of the Education for All Children Act passed in the United States in the 1970s, the least restrictive environment, now an acceptable international guideline, simply means the learning environment, in both the physical and theoretical sense, should include the minimum required adaptations and restrictions (Henley 1992). In maintaining this type of setting, the learning environment remains as free and unrestricted as possible and adaptations are made only when critically needed. In choice of experiences, the physical environment, special adaptations to media, technique, and teaching methods, educators should try their best to support an approach that emphasises freedom, individuality, and flexibility.

Task analysis

Task analysis refers to the breaking down and analysing of each step in a project or task. In task analysis, each step is mastered before moving on to the next step, educators are required to model each step, and to observe and take notes on the progress of each child (Anderson 1994). In special needs, task analysis takes into consideration the often overlooked fact that, for example, some children cannot even sit long enough to experience touching clay, never mind manipulate it. Most often associated with the teaching of simple art skills to children in primary and secondary school, in early childhood, task analysis, though perhaps not in such a prescribed form, is common practice.

Further considerations

Other practices strongly promoted in art education for children with special needs is an emphasis on learning through the senses, the use of a multi-sensory approach in teaching and transmitting knowledge, and the highlighting of the process. However, because we have supported and detailed these considerations throughout the first three chapters of this book, a further review of them is redundant. Suffice to say, the guiding principles that underpin our artistic experiences should be practised with all children – regardless of challenge or need; the only adjustments we should implement are those that will further normalise, support, and encourage advancement in and through art experiences.

Chapter 5

Putting it together:

Using the early learning goals for creative development

THE EARLY LEARNING GOALS

First issued by the Qualifications and Curriculum Authority (QCA) in 1999, the 'early learning goals' were reissued a year later in the publication entitled *Curriculum Guidance for the Foundation Stage* (QCA 2000) to include detailed guidance on how educators can successfully meet the illustrated early learning goals. Hodge refers to this publication as 'the core reference document for the successful implementation of the foundation stage from September 2000' (in QCA 2000: 2). The structure offered with this guidance provides staff with desperately needed objectives; the publication and subsequent implementation of these goals enable us to create art experiences and build an art curriculum with purpose and clarity.

What are the goals?

The Education Act 2002 extends England's National Curriculum to include the Foundation Stage, consequently the 'six areas of learning' listed are considered the statutory curriculum. It is within each of the areas of learning we find the early learning goals.

We begin with the six areas of learning as listed in QCA (2000):

*   Personal, social and emotional development
*   Communication, language and literacy
*   Mathematical development
*   Knowledge and understanding of the world
*   Physical development
*   Creative development.

As this book is about the visual arts, and the goals for creative development include art, as well as dance, music, imaginative and role play, we focus on this area of learning.

The area of creative development has five early learning goals organised into four 'aspects of learning'. The aspects of learning and the early learning goals within those aspects include the following:

Aspect of learning:
Exploring media and materials

Early learning goals:
1. Explore colour, texture, shape, form and space in two and three dimensions

Aspect of learning:
Music

Early learning goals:
2. Recognise and explore how sounds can be changed, sing simple songs from memory, recognise repeated sounds and sound patterns and match movements to music

Aspect of learning:
Imagination

Early learning goals:
3. Use their imagination in art and design, music, dance, imaginative and role play and stories

Aspect of learning:
Responding to experiences, and expressing and communicating ideas

Early learning goals:
4. Respond in a variety of ways to what they see, hear, smell, touch, and feel.
5. Express and communicate their ideas, thoughts and feelings by using a widening range of materials, suitable tools, imaginative and role play, movement, designing and making, and a variety of songs and musical instruments

(QCA 2000)

Each early learning goal is meant to be achieved by the end of the Foundation Stage. The idea is to master basic tasks within each goal and, by the end of the Foundation Stage, to offer children more complex opportunities to achieve the given goal.

With a careful review, it is obvious that the aspect of learning in the area of music is not intended for the visual arts. This does not mean, however, that at times we cannot make it applicable to the visual arts. With keen observation and accurate documentation, many experiences in the visual arts can be linked in some capacity to music. Taking this thought a step further, it is quite valid to say it is possible, through *thematic units* or *projects*, to integrate many of the early learning goals, from each area of learning, into worthwhile experiences. Nevertheless, while a brief discussion of theme and project work follows in this chapter, a full exploration of curriculum development utilising all of the learning areas would fill volumes. Hence, we continue with our focal point, the early learning goals for creative development. We start with the basics and look first at how creative development relates to the visual arts.

Creativity and the visual arts

The term creativity is repeatedly defined and redefined in educational literature. Lowenfeld and Brittain (1987: 74) point out: 'The definition of creativity depends upon who is doing the defining.' Valid definitions range from innovation, to the ability to make new connections and see obscure relationships, to simply thinking differently or being a 'divergent' thinker (ibid.). Though all of these definitions are certainly applicable to the word creative, it is hard to come up with one definition for a word that is changeable – its fundamental nature is active. To clarify, being creative means any number of things. It can mean seeing many different possibilities, coming up with new ideas, being original or inventive. However, because, in art, these behaviours will take place within experience, during the process, the meaning we attach to creativity will depend on the process the child is involved in. For example, children building with blocks may be creative because they are thinking of new ways to, perhaps, get the blocks to stand on top of one another. Creativity, in this case, can be defined as seeking new and inventive ways to work out problems. In another instance, children looking at and interpreting a painting may be creative because they are using a process that includes original thinking; using their imaginations to dream up a story about the person or object depicted. In this, creativity might be defined as employing imaginative thought. Creativity is part of the process. It does not have one fixed definition. Furthermore, similar to artistic experiences, creativity is dynamic. The definition constantly regenerates itself. In an earlier passage, Lowenfeld and Brittain (1987: 75) explain: 'The very act of creating can provide new insights and new knowledge for further action.'

Many often confuse art with creativity, with this in mind it is important to stress that while the act of creation can apply to making art and the making of art can sometimes be creative, the two are not synonymous. Lowenfeld and Brittain (1987) correctly argue that many art experiences are not at all creative, think of the teacher-directed art activity, and that creative thinking is not exclusive to art making, all disciplines require the ability to, perhaps, see relationships, or produce original thoughts, invent, and so forth. Art and creativity, instead of being used interchangeably, are better used in conjunction with one another. Art experiences are fuelled by creative behaviour: exploration, discovery, or perhaps the ability to see new solutions; and creativity is sometimes exemplified through a tangible outpouring or 'creation' that takes the form of an artistic product.

In art, creativity is experienced within the process and made visible in the art-work itself. It is both a driving force and, at the same time, an actual act. If educators want to encourage creativity within the visual arts, an emphasis on the process, as described in Chapter 2, intervention on the part of staff, and opportunities for children to partake in discovery, dialogue, and investigation are vital.

Goals for creative development and everyday art experiences

As we just learned, though we exercise creative thinking in most learning areas, creativity is often associated with the arts – the act of creation or of making something, the open-endedness of positive artistic experiences, the use of imagination, and the emphasis placed on the process are some of the many visual art characteristics that lead people to this association. The placement of the visual arts within the learning area of creative development is further evidence of this relationship. It is within this context that we look at ways in which the goals for creative development can be merged with everyday artistic experiences (including art making, aesthetic experiences, and encounters with art).

Two of the most practical and straightforward methods staff can use to tie the early learning goals for creative development in with children's experiences are using the goals as a guide, and supporting the 'emergence' of the goals within artistic experience.

Using the goals for creative development as a guide

Educators can quite straightforwardly base art experiences on the early learning goals for creative development. Even though we have explored at length the idea of the process and the flexibility staff must maintain in order to ensure relevant art learning, this does not mean that we dismiss goals and objectives. Goals are necessary in the formulation and execution of artistic experiences. Goals also provide staff with a wonderful guide. While our emphasis is placed on the process and on encouraging children to seek multiple solutions and see new possibilities, it remains the educator's responsibility to facilitate these actions and ensure that as the children explore they are successfully meeting goals along the way.

When devising opportunities for children to participate in artistic experiences, educators should turn to the early learning goals, and figure out how the goals can both serve the needs of the children and, at the same time, become an underlying objective of the experience (children's needs articulated through, for example dialogue and observation, and recorded in documentation). For instance, imagine children have just been to a museum and had the privilege of encountering a Sioux warrior's headdress. While the children viewed the headdress, staff may have overheard, and subsequently documented, some of the children talking about how a Native American, in this case a Sioux warrior, would act when wearing such a treasure. When staff revisit this documentation, they now use all the information they culled from this encounter and create for children a meaningful art experience based on the early learning goals for creative development. Perhaps, noticing the children's interest in role playing a Native American warrior, educators will base their next experience around the goal that states children use their imagination in art and design, music, dance, imaginative and role play, and stories. In the new experience, educators could encourage children to think of other textiles or objects that potentially change the wearer's behaviour – masks, costumes, and the like. Alternatively, they might have a new experience creating masks and using them in a role play. Figure 5.1 offers another example of how the goals can guide an experience.

Take a moment to note that merely fulfilling a goal does not constitute an artistic experience. Again, worthwhile artistic experiences are dynamic with learning leading to more learning; they house a valuable process; are fuelled by documentation, dialogue, and motivation; and they stem from both previous experiences and, most importantly, from the needs of the children. The early learning goals are there to provide basic guiding objectives and possible direction, they are not offered simply as a list of activities for children to engage in.

The emergence of goals within artistic experiences

This method of utilising the goals for creative development in artistic experiences is not quite as prescribed as the first approach. In basic terms, throughout the course

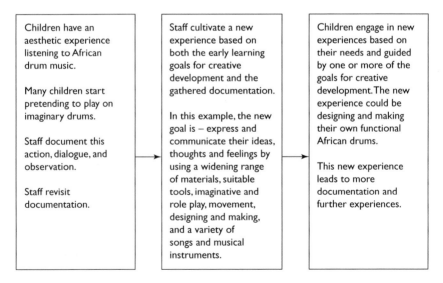

Children have an aesthetic experience listening to African drum music. Many children start pretending to play on imaginary drums. Staff document this action, dialogue, and observation. Staff revisit documentation.	Staff cultivate a new experience based on both the early learning goals for creative development and the gathered documentation. In this example, the new goal is – express and communicate their ideas, thoughts and feelings by using a widening range of materials, suitable tools, imaginative and role play, movement, designing and making, and a variety of songs and musical instruments.	Children engage in new experiences based on their needs and guided by one or more of the goals for creative development. The new experience could be designing and making their own functional African drums. This new experience leads to more documentation and further experiences.

Figure 5.1 Using the goals for creative development as a guide

of an experience, as staff observe and interact with children, topics, issues, and actions will occur or arise that may touch upon one of the early learning goals. When one of the goals is hinted at, or *emerges*, educators gently guide children to achieve success within that goal. For example, suppose children were working on collages and staff noticed children's interest in the textures seen and felt on the different scraps employed as collage media (this interest could be revealed in any number of ways, for instance, observed through the children's actions or overheard in dialogue). Educators well versed in the early learning goals would recognise that the goal stating explore colour, texture, shape, form and space in two or three dimensions would easily apply and, in an effort to enable children to successfully meet the early learning goal, this would be emphasised. This emphasis on the early learning goals could come in many forms. Staff could highlight the goal by prompting children to talk about the textures or educators could formulate a future lesson, after the collage experience, taking children outside to find textures in the natural environment. Figure 5.2 illustrates another example of this method.

Apart from how staff support the emergence of the goals, the most important part of this method is actually being aware of these excellent opportunities, and this awareness relies on intervention, dialogue, observation, and documentation. Additionally, in order for educators to successfully notice and accentuate goals, they must have a thorough working knowledge of the goals.

Staff should not just use one approach or the other. The methods work best in combination with each other. Here again we apply Schaefer and Cole's (1990: 6) idea of 'teachable moments', those moments where, with the main goals in mind, the adult presents extended learning opportunities. Using the early learning goals as a guide, staff absorb children in a new experience, as the new experience unfolds, and other early learning goals begin to emerge, staff highlight the

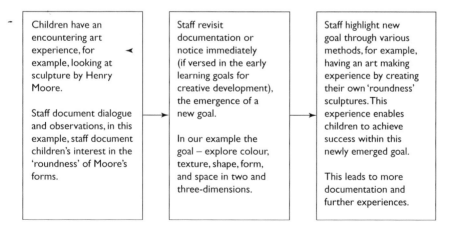

Figure 5.2 How goals for creative development can emerge within artistic experiences

emerging goal or goals, all the while maintaining a connection with the initial objectives.

As an example, we go back to the collage experience. Imagine the collage experience was created for children around the goal 'explore colour, texture, shape, form and space in two or three dimensions'. Say, during the course of the experience, staff observed children relating the patterns on the collage fabrics to a patterned African textile left in the dress-up box. This is the perfect teachable moment. With knowledge of the early learning goals, yet not forgetting to either fulfil or continue with the initial goal, staff now highlight a new objective, in this case the emerging goal or objective might be 'use their imagination in art and design, music, dance, imaginative and role play and stories'. Educators might, for instance, interest children in a further experience that involves the use of textiles in role play. They could ask children to use their imagination and come up with a story about the piece of African fabric, who wore it? What purpose did it serve? Children might design a pattern that represents their culture, or simply have an encounter comparing and contrasting textile patterns from two different cultures. Figure 5.3 offers another example. In fact, staff will soon realise the possibilities for new, connected, extended experiences are virtually limitless. Once started, if we guide experiences with underlying goals and, all the time, actively seek out emerging goals within the process, one simple experience could literally spark off hundreds more.

The goals for creative development and the other early learning goals

Through thematic units or projects, educators can integrate and link the early learning goals from each of the six areas. Although an in-depth investigation of these two methods is beyond the scope of this book, a curriculum that takes into account all the early learning goals is of the utmost importance to any educator's long-term planning. That being the case, a short description of the two methods follows. For more information, readers will want to consult the vast resources available to support them in the development of either thematic units or project work in their own classroom.

Thematic unit

A thematic unit is a unit of study based on a general topic. To develop a thematic unit staff plan lessons, built around a chosen subject, in each of the six areas of learning. The idea is to weave the topic into each area of learning, making learning within each discipline more understandable. For example, instead of children learning mathematical terms such as 'more' or 'less' as an isolated activity, in a thematic unit those terms would be learned as a result of an investigation into a topic. If the theme was 'weather', children might learn the terms 'more' or 'less' as they record the weekly rainfall on a chart. Instead of feeding

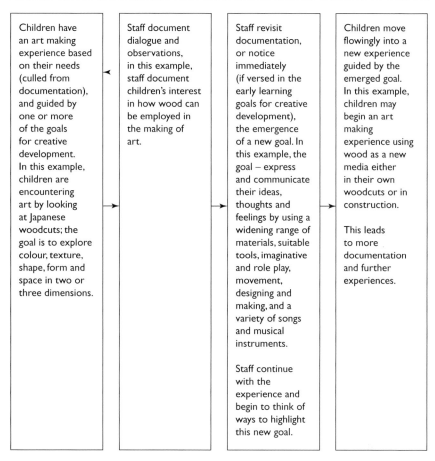

Children have an art making experience based on their needs (culled from documentation), and guided by one or more of the goals for creative development. In this example, children are encountering art by looking at Japanese woodcuts; the goal is to explore colour, texture, shape, form and space in two or three dimensions.	Staff document dialogue and observations, in this example, staff document children's interest in how wood can be employed in the making of art.	Staff revisit documentation, or notice immediately (if versed in the early learning goals for creative development), the emergence of a new goal. In this example, the goal – express and communicate their ideas, thoughts and feelings by using a widening range of materials, suitable tools, imaginative and role play, movement, designing and making, and a variety of songs and musical instruments. Staff continue with the experience and begin to think of ways to highlight this new goal.	Children move flowingly into a new experience guided by the emerged goal. In this example, children may begin an art making experience using wood as a new media either in their own woodcuts or in construction. This leads to more documentation and further experiences.

Figure 5.3 Employ both approaches. Use the goals for creative development as a guide, but also watch for and act upon the emergence of new goals within artistic experiences

children information, the information is embedded into lessons based on a specific theme.

There are many ways to construct thematic units – brainstorming, webbing of ideas, and the like will usually turn up more connections between areas of learning, and learning activities themselves, than an educator could possibly cover in the allotted time dedicated to the theme. The idea for a theme should stem from the desires and interests of the children. Some themes, such as 'animals', are very general, other themes, for example, 'trains' are a touch more specific. Dialogue, observation, and interaction with the children will guide educators to relevant theme topics.

Projects

Projects are thorough and comprehensive explorations into topics, ideas, or suggestions that are raised or culled through dialogue with children, in a review of documentation, or in our interactions with children during experiences. Describing the difference between projects and themes Katz (1994: 1) states: 'Related to project work are themes and units . . . However, in theme work children are rarely involved in posing questions to be answered or taking initiative for investigation on the topic.'

Projects form a major part of the aforementioned Reggio Emilia approach. Carlina Rinaldi, pedagogical director of Reggio Emilia schools, states:

> A project, which we view as a sort of adventure and research, can start through a suggestion from an adult, a child's idea, or from an event such as a snowfall or something else unexpected. But every project is based on the attention of the educators to what the children say and do, as well as what they do not say and do not do. The adults must allow enough time for the thinking and actions of children to develop.
>
> (Rinaldi 1998: 122–123)

Similar to artistic experiences, the course a project follows is steered by the process, propelled by the interests, needs, and discoveries of the children; again, these variables reveal themselves through documentation, prior experiences, dialogue, and observation. In addition, projects too, like artistic experiences, are dynamic, ideas leading to more ideas. Demanding the flexibility and adaptability of educators Rinaldi describes planning for projects,

> as a method of work in which the teachers lay out general educational objectives, but do not formulate the specific goals for each project or each activity in advance. Instead they formulate hypotheses of what could happen on the basis of their knowledge of the children and of previous experiences. Along with these hypotheses, they formulate objectives that are flexible and adapted to the needs and interests of the children. These interests and needs include those expressed by children at any time during the project as well as those the teachers infer and bring out as the work proceeds. A great deal of time and attention is given to this projection. It is repeated at many different points, both among teachers and with the children, in order to inform their future choices and decisions.
>
> (1998: 113)

Another difference between themes and projects is the nature of the topic being investigated (Katz 1994). Katz explains, 'Unlike themes and units, the topic of a project is a real phenomenon that children can investigate directly' (ibid.: 2). Ideas for projects constantly present themselves. For example, educators observing children may notice a repeated fascination with the way rocks, clouds, or even a puddle of spilled milk often looks like something else – a face, a horse, or perhaps a spider. Educators documenting the children's interest may conclude that children are engaging in metaphoric thinking. In an effort to support this type of thinking a project could be embarked upon using metaphors as the foundation. With the project idea in mind, staff begin to build the skeleton of the project, knowing it will be fleshed out and brought to life by the children's needs and discoveries as the project itself unfolds. While a thematic unit in this case may have focused on, possibly, rocks, and would have been planned in a more formal fashion, the project is more flexible and dynamic, planning happening throughout. The early learning goals both emerge throughout the course of a project and serve to guide experiences within the project.

Artistic experiences fit into, prompt, and can easily become a project or the basis of thematic units. Using thematic units or projects, the area of creative development blends naturally with the other areas of learning, resulting in a highly integrated early years curriculum.

REALISING ART EXPERIENCES

Using Part II

Part II of this book offers educators various artistic experiences that are linked to the early learning goals for creative development. As previously pointed out, plans are necessary if our objective is to offer children valuable artistic experiences; however, one must remember plans need to be flexible, adaptable, and in order for art experiences to be meaningful, they must stem from the needs of the child. Observation, documentation, motivation, dialogue, reflection on the tangible end product are required throughout each of the experiences both to uncover the children's needs and interests, and to enable staff and children to see the infinite possibilities and various educational directions that can be realised within each of the given experiences. When educators begin using some of the described lessons, applying the essential interactions, they will find that the potential for new artistic experiences is huge. An experience making clay tiles may turn up a deep interest in pattern work, a textile experience might reveal a fascination with, say, primitive dying methods, or an experience in quilting could demonstrate a love of functional art. In any case, with the educator's active role, the experiences offered in Part II, are just the beginning, in both theory and practice, each one leading to dozens more.

Implementing the experiences

The artistic experiences in Part II include suggestions for motivation and dialogue, and procedures for the lesson itself. Also included are general objectives in the form of the early learning goals and specific objectives presented as the ways in which the goals might be met, any background information needed, and, if necessary, adaptations for children with special needs. Readers may wish to refer to previous chapters for in-depth information on any of these components.

Prior to using the lessons staff should be aware of a few points:

1   *Not all of the early learning goals for creative development will be met with every lesson*: While it would not be impossible to link each goal with every lesson, it certainly is not important to do so. The idea is to achieve success within given goals. If we try to force too many goals into each lesson, there is a possibility children would not successfully realise even one.

    Some lessons will state a goal is fulfilled through, say, looking at the life of an artist, or engaging in role play. Remember, depending on where the experience leads, some of the goals stated may not be met. Goal realisation depends on how the experience unfolds. The listed fulfilments or specific objectives represent the many possibilities.

2   *Lessons should build on each other*: Refrain from teaching lessons that are developmentally inappropriate. For example, if an experience in Part II asks children to roll clay into a ball, and children have never even touched clay, suggesting that they actually make something out of it, in this case a ball, would be incorrect.

    In order to avoid the possibility of this happening, educators should do two things. First, begin by implementing the 'initial media experiences' found in the beginning of Part II: Exploring Clay (Experience No. 1), Exploring Paint (Experience No. 2), and so forth. These lessons build the foundation for future artistic endeavours. Next, always be sure to refer to the section entitled 'When' in each of the experiences. This section informs the educator of any prerequisite experiences children must complete before starting the given lesson.

    Finally, the experiences, though created for children in the Foundation Stage, can be adapted to many levels of maturation. In fact, educators should be aware that even within the Foundation Stage, many developmental levels are present and adjustments to the experiences offered are necessary.

3   *Background information*: Any necessary background information, for example, art historical facts, or technical terms, depending on the information needed, is offered as a reference book or website address. It is true websites change and books go out of print; however, the information required is quite basic and alternative resources on the subjects, besides those described, are plentiful. Educators should turn to reference materials before beginning any of the experiences, as the more educators know about art the more the possibilities to extend or create further art endeavours.

    Finally, refer to the Appendices of this book for information on art materials, a brief art history background, museums, professional organizations, children and adult art books, and websites.

4   *Art making experiences*: Because art making is more concrete in nature than the other two forms of experience (aesthetic experiences and encounters with art), it will appear that the lessons in Part II are chiefly art making experiences. However, we have learned that all three forms of art experience are interrelated. Art making experiences incorporating encounters with art, encounters with art involving aesthetic experiences, or an aesthetic experience involving art making – all three stimulate each other. This relationship becomes obvious as staff implement the lessons. Throughout the course of any of the experiences in Part II, children will both encounter art and have a multitude of aesthetic experiences; furthermore, educators will find that some (certainly not all) of these opportunities are highlighted or suggested within the given experiences.

Remember, art making, aesthetic experiences, and encounters with art *together* form an educational arts programme. An arts curriculum that only focuses on art making experiences would not be considered comprehensive, holistic, or educational. For more information on art making, art encounters, and aesthetic experiences refer to Chapters 2 and 3.

5   *Length of time*: The time children and staff spend on an experience depends entirely on where the process leads them. Some lessons may take one to two hours spread over two days, while others can take up to two hours a day for a month. The hope is that these experiences lead to so many other ideas, it becomes hard to see where one experience ends and another begins.

6   *The lessons are just the beginning*: The offered lessons are only the beginning; think of them as sparks – sparks that have the potential to branch out in infinite directions. If educators take an active role in the children's experiences and utilise previously discussed tools such as observation, dialogue, or documentation, it is quite probable that any one part of the described experiences or, indeed, the entire experience itself will lead to more future adventures than educators and children could possibly imagine.

As educators leap into Part II and set off on new exciting artistic experiences, continue to use this book as a guide; refer to it on a regular basis throughout the creation and subsequent practice of appropriate and beneficial art in the early years methodology.

Ideas into practice:

Artistic experiences for the Foundation Stage

Initial clay experience

EXPLORING CLAY

When

This experience is an initial introduction to clay; a shorter version of the experience can be practised before all clay activities.

Materials

1 Air-dry or natural clay.
2 Paper plates (or other cardboard material to rest clay on).
3 Small bowls with water.
4 Selection of wooden clay tools (can use wooden spoons, forks, and tongue depressors).
5 For later introduction, educators may wish to have available: natural materials (rocks, leaves, twigs, bark). If in an urban environment staff can use textures found in the classroom such as corrugated cardboard or objects found in the environment such as wire, rope, or netting.
6 Photos, reproductions, and any background information (Dogon houses, Greek pottery; read through experience).

Motivation

There is very little motivation in initial experiences. Our objective is to let the children simply explore the media. Nevertheless, some motivation may include:

1 Show children a lump of clay; model smelling, touching, and manipulating the media.
2 Think about where clay comes from. Go outside and look for clay in the earth. When outside, collect objects, both natural and human made, to use in your clay exploration.
3 Bring objects made out of clay (tiles, pots, dishes) into the class. Have children examine the objects.

4 Talk about why clay is so important; its uses in storage, cooking, and even shelter. Encounter art: look at the clay storage pots of ancient Greece and the clay houses of the African Dogon people. See Figure Ex 1.1.

5 Have a lump of clay on a table, give children time to look at the clay under a magnifying glass or a microscope.

6 Leave a lump of clay in a glass bowl with water, leave another lump of clay next to the bowl on the table. Encourage children to observe what happens to both the clay in the water and the clay drying out on the table.

7 Demonstrate how we care for clay.

Art making

Many children will not have used clay before. The intention of this experience is to allow children to explore clay through the senses. The procedures are quite simple:

1 Give each child a lump of clay or let children take their own lump of clay out of the bag or container.

2 Have an aesthetic experience and ask children to feel the clay, smell the clay, and explore the clay through the senses.

3 Encourage children to pound, stretch, and manipulate the clay.

4 Introduce water, ask children to wet their hands and touch the clay.

5 Bring some natural or found objects and wooden clay tools to the work area. Model using the tools or objects to make marks and impressions in the clay.

6 Ask children to flatten the clay, and if ready, to roll or pinch the clay. Model breaking it apart, building it up, rolling, pinching, and pounding the clay.

Possible discussion or dialogue

1 Engage children in a discussion about clay. Ask children if they know what it is.

2 Ask children where they think clay comes from. Seek out prior knowledge, and dispel myths.

3 Discuss the uses of clay in both art and everyday living. Talk about the different cultures that use clay.

4 Talk about clay items in the classroom, in their homes, in the natural environment. How are these items different to the lump of clay in our hand?

5 While using the clay, employ expressive terminology to describe what the clay feels, smells, looks like. Encourage children to do the same, to verbalise their response to the clay – is it sticky, hard, cold?

6 Discuss what happens when we put water on the clay. Talk about what happens when the clay dries out.

7 When using tools or objects to make impressions in the clay, ask children to describe the marks they make, the textures, or patterns formed.

Figure Ex. 1.1   This large clay vessel resembles the *pithos* used for storage in ancient
            Greece
Source: Courtesy collection M. Eglinton, tribalhouse.net.

8 Describe how marks made by tools or objects are different to the ones made by our fingers and fists.

9 Discuss how nature provides us with many of the tools necessary to create art. Discuss the role nature played in our art making.

10 Talk about any of the visual products created because of the exploration. Can you tell where you pounded the clay? Do some of the impressions left in the clay remind us of the tool used to make that impression?

11 Discuss proper clean-up and care for clay, clay tools, and natural objects.

FULFILMENT OF THE EARLY LEARNING GOALS FOR CREATIVE DEVELOPMENT

Goal

•   Explore colour, texture, shape, form and space in two and three dimensions.

Fulfilment

•   Children explore the properties of clay through the senses.
•   Children discover texture when they use objects to make impressions in the soft clay.

Goal

•   Use their imagination in art and design, music, dance, imaginative and role play and stories.

Fulfilment

•   Children explore the uses of clay in other cultures.
•   Children imagine what it would be like to live in a clay house.

Goals

•   Respond in a variety of ways to what they see, hear, smell, touch, and feel.
•   Express and communicate their ideas, thoughts and feelings by using a widening range of materials, suitable tools, imaginative and role play, movement, designing and making, and a variety of songs and musical instruments.

Fulfilment

•   Children begin to explore the use of natural and man-made tools and objects in the forming of expression.

- Children respond to the clay by exploring it through the senses.
- Children discuss the texture created by the natural/man-made objects.
- Children talk about the feeling, smell, and look of clay.
- Children observe and study the properties of clay.

Background information

1 The UNESCO's World Heritage has information on the clay houses of the Dogon people. See website: http://whc.unesco.org.

2 A full account of ancient Greek pottery is found in most Greek art and archaeology books including, J.G. Pedley, *Greek Art and Archaeology*, Prentice Hall (1993).

Educators should pay particular attention to the *pithos* – the large storage vessels where, for example, vast quantities of olive oil would be stored.

Special needs adaptation

This experience does not require any adaptations for children with special needs.

Initial painting experience

EXPLORING PAINT

When

This experience is an initial introduction to painting; a shorter version of the experience can be practised before all painting activities.

Materials

1 Finger paint (finger paint is a wonderful medium because it is thick and dripless). If unable to get finger paint, staff can use thick school paint. In an exploratory activity of this nature, one or two available colours will suffice.
2 Large white paper.
3 Brushes (various sizes).
4 For later introduction, educators may wish to have available twigs, sticks, and other tools with which children can apply paint.
5 Paper can be taped onto a low table or pinned to an easel, observe where children are most comfortable.
6 Photos, reproductions, and any background information (Wassily Kandinsky, Jackson Pollock; read through experience).

Motivation

Initially, the paint itself will motivate; additional motivational activities may include:

1 Look at painted surfaces both inside and outside the classroom.
2 Have an aesthetic experience, show children the paints. Do not touch them yet, just look at them, the colours, texture, shine. Smell the paints, and finally feel the paints. Stick your fingers in the pot of paint; rub the paint over your palms.
3 Encounter art; introduce children to a painting by an artist. Look at the work of Jackson Pollock or Wassily Kandinsky.

4 Explore the reasons for using paint.

5 Examine paint under a magnifying glass or a microscope.

6 Observe what happens both when paint dries and when water is added to it.

7 After using fingers to make marks with the paint, begin studying the paintbrushes. Encourage children to hold a brush, to dip it in the paint pot, to make a mark on the paper with it.

8 Explore other ways to apply paint. Look around the room and in nature for objects that act like brushes.

9 Compare and contrast the mediums paint and clay.

10 Demonstrate how we care for paint and our paintings.

Art making

Many children will not have touched paint before, be advised that some may not like the feeling. The intention of this experience is to allow children to explore the properties of paint through the senses:

1 Set each child up with a pot of finger paint and a large piece of white paper.

2 Have children begin by exploring the paint with their fingers. Ask children to discover the paint through their senses.

3 Encourage children to make marks on the paper with the paint from their fingers.

4 After using their fingers, possibly at a later time, ask children to try to hold a brush. Model this action.

5 Children can then use brushes of various sizes to make marks.

6 Explore other ways of applying paint to the paper. Try twigs, leaves, sponges, and so forth.

Possible discussion or dialogue

1 Talk to children about paint. Ask children if they have ever seen wet paint before. What about dry paint?

2 Talk about painted surfaces, show children how a surface changes when it is painted.

3 Discuss the abstract paintings of artists such as Jackson Pollock or Wassily Kandinsky. Look at the marks they make. Ask children how they think those marks were made – with their fingers? Brushes? Twigs?

4 Discuss the properties of paint when it is wet. Is it smooth? Bumpy? Watery? Soft? How does it smell? Look? Feel? Encourage the use of descriptive language.

5 While children are using the paint, engage them in a dialogue. What are they thinking? Are they trying to make symbols? Are they more interested in the physical properties of paint? Seek out their developmental level.

6 Talk about the different ways we can apply paint. When using fingers, talk about how it relates to using our hands when we use clay. If using brushes, talk about

how the size has an effect on the marks being made. If using natural objects talk about the texture of the impressions.

7 Discuss how to care for paint, painting tools, and the paintings themselves.

8 After the experience, discuss some of the visual works. Review what tools were used to make certain shapes or marks. Talk about how the painting looks different when it dries.

FULFILMENT OF THE EARLY LEARNING GOALS FOR CREATIVE DEVELOPMENT

Goal

• Explore colour, texture, shape, form and space in two and three dimensions.

Fulfilment

• Children explore the properties of paint through the senses.
• Children begin to understand shape and texture by employing various tools for the application of paint.
• Children feel texture when applying paint with their fingers, and running their hands over the final dried painting.
• Children begin to understand space when shapes and marks begin to fill the paper.

Goal

• Use their imagination in art and design, music, dance, imaginative and role play and stories.

Fulfilment

• Children use imaginative and innovative thinking when utilising various tools with which to apply paint.
• Children may create stories about their marks, shapes, or final paintings.

Goal

• Respond in a variety of ways to what they see, hear, smell, touch, and feel.
• Express and communicate their ideas, thoughts and feelings by using a widening range of materials, suitable tools, imaginative and role play, movement, designing and making, and a variety of songs and musical instruments.

Fulfilment

- Children start to understand how to communicate ideas through artistic media.
- Children begin to explore the use of natural and man-made tools and objects in the formation of expression.
- Children start to talk about and reflect upon both their artistic experiences and subsequent visual products.
- Children respond to paint by exploring it through the senses.
- Children discuss the texture created by the natural/man-made objects.
- Children talk about the feeling, smell, and look of paint.
- Children observe and study the properties of paint.

Background information

Jackson Pollock (1912–1956), abstract expressionist and action painter, and Wassily Kandinsky (1866–1944), expressionist painter, are two of the many artists staff may wish to introduce to children in any exploratory painting experience. These two particular artists are highlighted here because of their exciting compositions and abstract style. Educators can find out more about these two artists by referencing most twentieth-century art history books, or encyclopedias and CD-ROMs (see Appendix 4 for resources); Kandinsky features in the earlier part of the century; Pollock in the middle to early second half. Both artists' brief biographies, examples of their work, and links to related sites can be found on the Artcyclopedia website: http://www.artcyclopedia.com put in a search for Pollock or Kandinsky.

Special needs adaptation

Though this experience does not require any adaptations for children with special needs, educators should take into account physical development before encouraging children to use paintbrushes.

Initial printing experience

EXPLORING PRINTING

When

This experience is an initial introduction to printing; educators may wish to remind children of this experience before beginning any advanced printing lessons.

Note: Use this experience after the Initial clay experience (Experience No. 1) and Initial painting experience (Experience No. 2) as both mediums are employed in this lesson.

Materials

1 Finger paint (finger paint is a great initial medium to use in printing) or block printing ink (found in any craft shop, make sure it is water-based). If unable to get either of these paints, staff can use normal school paint with a touch of PVA glue mixed in to thicken it up.
2 Soft air-dry or natural clay.
3 Large white paper.
4 Various natural and man-made objects such as twigs, acorns, pine cones, sponges, netting, wooden blocks, and so forth.

Motivation

The process of printing is incredibly magical – motivating. Yet, there are still some ways to motivate children and further enhance this wonderful experience.

1 Before talking about printing as a form of art making, engage in an aesthetic experience by taking children outside, and find some wet sand or mud to press your hands or feet into. Talk about the impression or 'print' left behind. If there is no sand or mud, or if the educational setting is purely urban, educators can bring in a tray of wet sand.
2 Look for animal prints, and talk about places you see prints, for example, a dog sometimes leaves a muddy paw print on the floor, or a bear will leave a footprint in the snow (see Figure Ex 3.1).

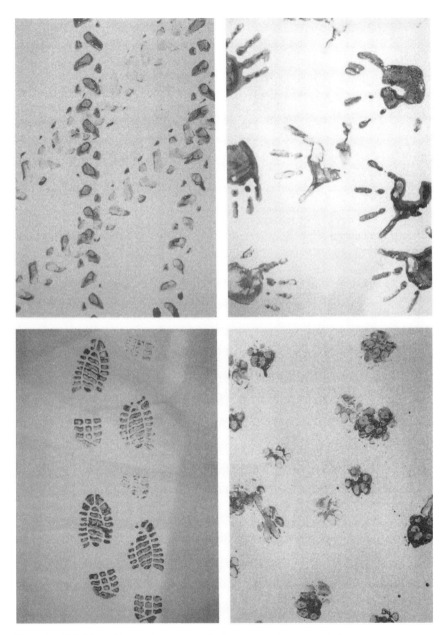

Figure Ex. 3.1   Tyres, hands, feet, even a dog's paws can leave a 'print'
Source: Photo by M. Eglinton.

3 When outside, ask children to begin collecting objects that have textures on them, look for pine cones, bark, leaves.

4 Show children how paint can be used to leave a print. Model dipping your finger into a paint pot and making a print on paper.

5 Explore other ways to make prints. Look at a natural object such as a pine cone, model for children dipping a pine cone in paint and making a print with it on clean paper.

6 Study making prints on other surfaces. Just like a print left in snow or mud, explore leaving a print in clay. Demonstrate making a print onto a clay surface.

7 Have an aesthetic experience looking at fingers under a magnifying glass. Study the lines of the fingerprint.

Art making

The main purpose of this activity is to enable children to understand the idea of leaving or making a print. This experience can be visited repeatedly using various media, textures, and surfaces:

1 Encourage each child to dip just one finger in a shallow pot of finger paint. Ask children to press their paint soaked finger onto the paper.

2 Continue step 1 using all of the fingers, a fist, or the child's palm.

3 Bring out some soft clay. Ask children to press one finger into the clay, all their fingers, their fist, palm.

4 Educators may now wish to bring out the natural and man-made objects. Press some objects into the soft clay and study the print (see Figure Ex. 3.2). Coat some of the objects with paint and press them on clean white paper, again, discover the print left behind.

Possible discussion or dialogue

1 Talk to the children about fingerprints and footprints. Ask children if they can show you what they think a finger or footprint is.

2 Discuss places you find prints – in the mud, on the floor, on a couch, in the sand. Talk about where prints come from – animals, humans, objects, the rain?

3 Explore and discuss a person's fingerprint. What does it look like, how can we get it onto paper?

4 Talk about what happens when we put paint on our finger and press it onto paper. Does it show our fingerprint?

5 Discuss how we can leave a print on clay. Do we need to use paint? Can we leave an impression without paint? Does the clay have to be soft or hard in order for us to leave an impression?

6 Talk about what happens when we press our fingers or hands into clay. Do we press differently when we make a print than when we pound, roll, or play with clay? Do we need to press hard or soft to make a print?

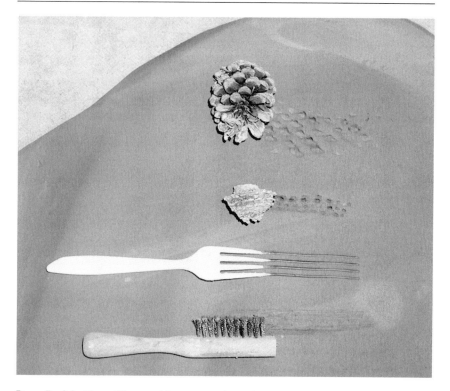

Figure Ex. 3.2 Many different objects can make an impression or print in clay
Source: Photo by M. Eglinton.

7 Engage in dialogue about the various textures of the natural and man-made objects. Think about the kind of print they will leave. Compare the prints objects leave with the objects themselves, for example, does a print of a pine cone look like a pine cone?

8 Talk about all of the final prints, reflect on the process, and discuss what else can be printed.

FULFILMENT OF THE EARLY LEARNING GOALS FOR CREATIVE DEVELOPMENT

Goal

• Explore colour, texture, shape, form and space in two and three dimensions.

Fulfilment

- Children explore the various textures of objects.
- Children transform three-dimensional form into a two-dimensional image or print.

Goal

- Use their imagination in art and design, music, dance, imaginative and role play and stories.

Fulfilment

- Children think about sequences; how a print was left, an impression was made.
- They think about cause and effect.

Goal

- Respond in a variety of ways to what they see, hear, smell, touch, and feel.
- Express and communicate their ideas, thoughts and feelings by using a widening range of materials, suitable tools, imaginative and role play, movement, designing and making, and a variety of songs and musical instruments.

Fulfilment

- Children respond to the impressions they leave.
- Children feel the different textures left on the clay, and see the textures left on paper.
- Children begin to see the uses of printing as a way to communicate ideas.
- Children will begin to explore the use of natural and man-made objects in the formation of expression.

Special needs adaptation

There is no background information or special needs adaptations in this experience.

Initial construction experience

EXPLORING CONSTRUCTION

When

This experience is an initial introduction to construction. This experience is usually encountered daily in most Foundation Stage environments; however, it is included here to ensure that children encounter this initial experience before educators think about embarking on more complex construction experiences, for example, sculptures fabricated using recycled products.

Provided materials are readily available and easily accessible, children can participate in this experience any time.

Materials

1 Boxes (various sizes).
2 Wooden or Styrofoam blocks.

Motivation

Initially, the simple act of constructing will most likely provide ample motivation. However, for additional encouragement educators may:

1 Model stacking boxes on top of each other, forming a shape or structure.
2 Look at parts of furniture, a house, a bird's nest. Think about how together all the parts form a whole.

Art making

Most children will spontaneously begin stacking or constructing if boxes or blocks are available. Encourage this behaviour by modelling it:

1 Give each child various blocks or boxes. Make sure boxes are small enough for tiny hands.

2 Show children how the boxes or blocks can sit on top of one another. Ask children to stack their boxes or blocks.

3 Remind children that there are other ways, besides stacking, we can use to put our blocks or boxes together. Ask children to think about the other ways to fit the boxes or blocks together.

Possible discussion or dialogue

1 Talk to children about parts and wholes. Encourage them to think about how the boxes or blocks look different when they are apart than when they are together. Ask children to describe the difference. Are they smaller when they are apart? Can you see every side of the block or box when it is alone? What about when they are stacked?

2 Discuss the simple forms that can be made in construction. We can make a tall 'line', a wide short box, and so forth. Have children think about how much space the different constructions take up. For example, does a tall tower use up more space than a low rectangular form?

3 Talk about the final constructions as though they were permanent structures.

4 Knock the constructions down. How do they look different now? What kind of new shapes or forms can we make? What took longer, building it or knocking it down? Which did we enjoy more the building or the knocking down? Why?

FULFILMENT OF THE EARLY LEARNING GOALS FOR CREATIVE DEVELOPMENT

Goal

- Explore colour, texture, shape, form and space in two and three dimensions.

Fulfilment

- Children explore the idea of shape and form in space.
- Children think about how much space is used by forms.
- Children explore three-dimensional form.

Goal

- Use their imagination in art and design, music, dance, imaginative and role play and stories.

Fulfilment

- Children think about 'what will happen next'.

- Children possibly make up stories about their constructions. Constructions become houses, backdrops, and scenery for role play.

Goal

- Respond in a variety of ways to what they see, hear, smell, touch, and feel.
- Express and communicate their ideas, thoughts and feelings by using a widening range of materials, suitable tools, imaginative and role play, movement, designing and making, and a variety of songs and musical instruments.

Fulfilment:

- Children begin to see construction as a way to communicate ideas and give form to expression.
- Children employ the proper media for construction, and learn what will and will not fit, work, or be suitable to the intended construction.

Background information

There is no necessary background information for this experience.

Special needs adaptation

This experience does not require any adaptations for children with special needs, however, as this lesson is very physical, educators should aim to provide media that is appropriate to each child's level of physical development.

Line and art elements

EXPLORING LINES

When

Only use this experience after children have already begun exploring the possibilities of drawing.

Materials

1 Chalk for drawing outside.
2 Large white paper.
3 Thick-nib felt tips.

Motivation

There are many ways to study the art element line. Educators might turn to nature for inspiration, or may wish to look at the more emotional side of lines, in other words, how lines can portray an emotion, for example, a zigzag line appears angry. This lesson touches upon both ideas, however, educators should eventually use both in two separate experiences.

1 Introduce children to the idea of line, search the room and look for lines (doorframes, pencils, and so forth).
2 Go on a walk and make looking for lines in the natural environment an aesthetic experience. Look at telephone wires, branches, even the lines that make up the 'skeleton' of a leaf or lines within an insect's wing. Encourage observation and keen visual sensitivity (see Figure Ex. 5.1).
3 Collect lines that have fallen to the ground, such as sticks, leaves, flower stems, and bring them into the classroom. Leave them out in the room with a magnifying glass for sensitive observation.
4 Inside think about the many types of lines. Draw some lines for children. Think variety – vary thickness, length, direction, and so forth (see Figure Ex. 5.2).

Figure Ex. 5.1 Hone visual perception and awareness, seek out lines in the environment
Source: Photo by M. Eglinton.

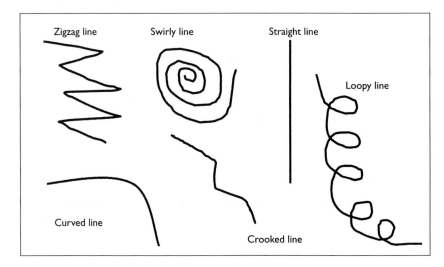

Figure Ex. 5.2 Line types

5 Draw lines for children that have 'personality', try to envision a happy line, an angry line, a sad line, etc. Lines will vary in thickness, darkness, direction (see Figure Ex. 5.3).

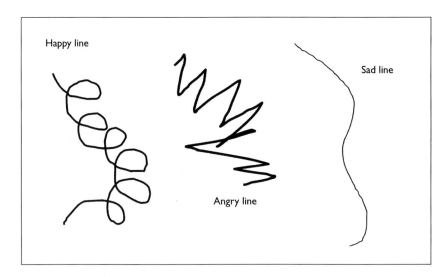

Figure Ex. 5.3 Line personalities

6 Get some chalk, go outside, and make some big lines on the pavement. If there is no pavement available, take some sticks or use fingers to make lines in sand, mud, or in the classroom sandpit. Vary thickness, direction, make up a story about your line; pretend your line is a car, dog, person – where is it going?

7 Roll a wheel, either the wheels on a child's bike or a single wheel you bring in, through a puddle. Look at the lines or line that forms.

8 Try to find the lines on our bodies. Look at fingers, arms, legs, veins.

9 Try to make ourselves into lines. Try being a straight line, a curved line, even a happy line.

Art making

Much of the motivation listed in this lesson works as an art making experience, or as aesthetic experiences. For example, going outside to draw big lines on the pavement can be an incredible art experience. However, if educators wish to take the lesson further they can expand either on the idea of line personalities or on the idea of lines in nature. Both ideas are outlined in this section.

For line personalities:

1   After a long discussion and motivation about line personalities, ask children what they would look like if they were a 'sad' line, a 'happy' line, and an 'angry' line. Have children draw their responses on large white paper. Note, younger children may not understand this concept, in which case just drawing lines or making marks is a valuable experience.

2   On new paper, older children may want to draw a line story using various lines. For example, I woke up and was tired (draw a tired line), and then I was happy (draw a happy line), now I am angry (draw an angry line). Younger children may just try a variety of different lines or may want simply to make marks.

Lines from nature:

1   Arrange some of the 'natural lines' collected outside (sticks, stems, branches). Study their thickness, length, direction. Are they curvy? Straight?

2   On big white paper, draw some of the natural lines. Start with a big branch or stick. Vary the thickness and copy the direction. Continue with the other natural treasures.

Possible discussion or dialogue

1 Talk to children about the art element line. Seek out prior knowledge, if they cannot point to a line in the room, ask them to draw one in the air with their finger.

2 While on your walk outside, discuss with children all the lines in the natural and formed environment. Model keen visual sensitivity; talk about finding lines in places we never thought to look, such as under the dirt (look for earthworms) or

within tree bark. Also point out some of the more obvious man-made lines, look for drainage pipes or telephone poles.

3 Talk about the many line types; explain to the children that lines are not just straight, that they can vary in many ways, for example, thickness, direction. When drawing the different line varieties for children, ask children to point out the differences.

4 Engage in dialogue about line personalities. Show children a happy or sad line (remember there is not a right or wrong interpretation of a so-called happy or sad line).

5 When outside drawing on the pavement, model for children talking aloud while drawing your line. Make up a story about your line, for example, you can say 'I am a car going very fast', or 'I am walking to the shop to buy some milk'. By modelling this type of narrative dialogue, we encourage children to talk about their work as it unfolds.

6 When rolling a wheel through water, talk about the line left on the pavement. If you have done the Initial printing experience (Experience No. 3), you may wish to relate the tyre mark with a type of print. Otherwise, comment on the direction and thickness of the lines that form.

7 When children create their own line personality compositions, educators should again encourage dialogue. Ask children to describe their line, listen for stories about their lines.

8 If drawing lines from nature, talk to children first about the natural line they have chosen to draw. Ask children questions that make them think about the physical properties of the line, for example, is it a wavy line? A 'heavy' or 'fat' line?

9 Reflect and respond to the finished line creations. For example, ask children how they achieved thickness, did they press harder on the paper?

FULFILMENT OF THE EARLY LEARNING GOALS FOR CREATIVE DEVELOPMENT

Goal

• Explore colour, texture, shape, form and space in two and three dimensions.

Fulfilment

• Children explore both two- and three-dimensional line types.

Goal

• Use their imagination in art and design, music, dance, imaginative and role play and stories.

Fulfilment

- Children make up stories about their lines.
- Children think about sequencing.

Goal

- Respond in a variety of ways to what they see, hear, smell, touch, and feel.
- Express and communicate their ideas, thoughts and feelings by using a widening range of materials, suitable tools, imaginative and role play, movement, designing and making, and a variety of songs and musical instruments.

Fulfilment

- Children respond both physically and visually to objects discovered in nature.
- Children begin to understand the element of line as a tool in the formation of their visual expressions.
- Children see both natural and man-made objects as source of inspiration and as a medium in their visual creations.

Background information and special needs adaptation

In this experience, there is no background information or special needs adaptations.

Clay and craft I

CLAY PINCH POTS

When

Use this experience only after children are capable of rolling clay into a ball. Before any clay experience, educators may wish to engage children in a short version of Initial clay experience (Experience No. 1).

Materials

1 Air-dry or natural clay.
2 Paper plates (or other cardboard material to rest clay on).
3 Small bowls with water.
4 If children wish to decorate their pots, educators may wish to have available: natural materials (rocks, leaves, twigs, bark) or if in an urban environment, use textures found in the classroom such as corrugated cardboard or objects found in the urban environment such as wire, rope, or netting.
5 Selection of wooden clay tools (can use wooden spoons, forks, and tongue depressors).
6 Mixture of PVA glue and water (ratio one-part glue/three-parts water), and brushes to apply the mixture.
7 Photos, reproductions, and any background information (Native American pottery, pueblo; read through experience). See Figure Ex. 6.1.

Motivation

1 Show children the clay, remind children of what they learned about clay in their initial clay explorations.
2 Show children 'container' objects made out of clay (bowls, vases, boxes). Look around the room for other objects that hold things.
3 Take a walk outside, repeat the motivation from the Initial clay experience, for example, look for clay, and gather textures.

Figure Ex. 6.1   Native American pot from Acoma Pueblo, New Mexico
Source: Photo courtesy G. Johnson, talaya.net.

4 While on your walk, look for container-shaped objects. Think about a bird's nest, a curved leaf with a raindrop in it. Model visual sensitivity; collect some of these objects for classroom exploration.

5 Encounter art: introduce children to Native American Indian art. Show pictures of Native American pots. Think about how they gathered the clay, what the pottery was used for (Figure Ex. 6.1).

6 Role play life as a Native American potter: finding, preparing, and shaping the clay, using the finished pots to drink from, store food. Think about life on a Pueblo (a Native American settlement).

7 After making the pots, continue motivating by taking a second nature walk. On this nature walk collect interesting textured objects children would like to use to decorate their pots with.

8 Use the media as a motivator, allow children ample time before forming their pots to pound, explore, and reacquaint themselves with clay.

Art making

1 Give children time to physically discover the clay again. Encourage sensory exploration.

2 After this initial exploration, ask children to roll a piece of clay (approximate size of their fist) into a ball. This step may take some time, for some children it may be the whole experience. Try to make this single step into an aesthetic experience, feel the 'roundness' of the ball, the coolness of the clay.

3 When children have successfully accomplished that skill demonstrate pushing your thumb into (not through) the centre of the pot. Encourage children to do the same with their ball of clay.

4 Model for children forming the pot by 'pinching' the sides of the pot between your thumbs in the centre and your fingers on the outside; enable children to do the same (see Figure Ex. 6.2). If clay seems to be drying out, allow children to sprinkle a touch of water over the surface of their pot.

5 After making the pots, talk to children about decorating. Using objects collected on a nature walk, model pressing textures into or making marks onto the pot. Children may or may not want to decorate their pots.

6 To ensure durability, educators may wish to cover the pots with a mixture of PVA and water.

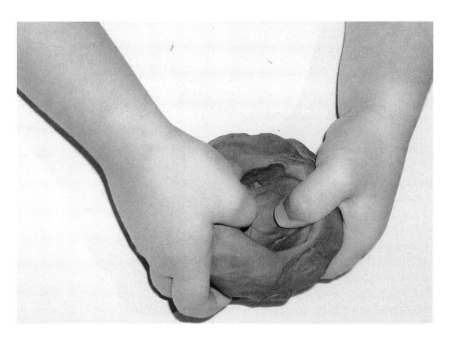

Figure Ex. 6.2 Making a pinch pot
Source: Photo by M. Eglinton.

Possible discussion or dialogue

1 Talk about the properties of clay, encourage children to articulate their feelings about the medium. Do they like the way it feels? How does it feel? Look? Smell?

2 Discuss the container. What is a container? Where are containers in the room? Do containers always have a lid? Do containers have to hold a lot? Are there any tiny containers in the room? Can we make our hand into a container?

3 On your initial walk outside, look for containers in nature. Call attention to holes in the ground, animal dwellings, and not so obvious containers, for example, a curved leaf or a beehive.

4 Engage in dialogue about natural and human-made containers. Encourage children to collect containers, understand their various shapes, and think about their uses.

5 Discuss the idea of a pot as a container. Bring in some pots from home and talk about their uses. Think about what pots are made out of. Talk about how some pots are made from clay.

6 Show children some examples of Native American clay pots. Discuss where the clay is from, how it is shaped. Think about what they used their pots for (cooking, storage, drinking).

7 When making the pinch pots, encourage children to talk about what their pots will be used for. Discuss the size of their pot, how it will be useful, talk about the medium, is clay a good material for making pots? Talk about the skills and the process they are using to form the pots. Can they roll the clay into a ball? Is the clay soft enough to pinch?

8 Talk to children about decorating their pots. Think about why people decorate objects. Educators may wish to show children some examples of decorated pots.

9 While on a walk collecting objects for decorating pots with, remind children of the initial printing exploration in this book. Discuss the different marks various textures left in the clay. Educators may even wish to refer to the finished work from those initial explorations, and ask children, 'Do you remember what object made that impression?', 'Was it prickly?' 'Or smooth?'

10 When children begin decorating their pots, engage them in dialogue about the textures, how the textures look on the pots.

11 Reflect on the experience, the process of making pots, and respond to the visual works.

12 At the end of this experience, educators can begin talking to children about how pots get hard. Talk about cooking the pots in a fire or *kiln*. Introduce proper terminology.

FULFILMENT OF THE EARLY LEARNING GOALS FOR CREATIVE DEVELOPMENT

Goal

- Explore colour, texture, shape, form and space in two and three dimensions.

Fulfilment

- Children explore the properties of clay through the senses.
- Children discover texture when they use objects to decorate the clay pots.
- Children explore shape and form when they investigate containers and pots.

Goal

- Use their imagination in art and design, music, dance, imaginative and role play and stories.

Fulfilment

- Children imagine the uses of clay in other cultures.
- Children role play life as a Native American potter.
- Children think about uses for their pots.

Goal

- Respond in a variety of ways to what they see, hear, smell, touch, and feel.
- Express and communicate their ideas, thoughts and feelings by using a widening range of materials, suitable tools, imaginative and role play, movement, designing and making, and a variety of songs and musical instruments.

Fulfilment

- Children respond to the clay by exploring it through the senses.
- Children discuss the texture created by the natural/man-made objects.
- Children use touch and visual sensitivity in the formation of a clay pot.
- Children use media to create both an artistic and a useful object.
- Children begin to explore the use of natural objects in the formation of expression.
- Children use artistic media as the basis of their role play.

Background information

There are vast amounts of information available on Native American art. This information comes in the form of websites and books easily accessible from a local library. Some websites and sources include: The Internet Public Library http://www.ipl.org/ readers should click on the link for Exhibits, and then Pueblo Pottery. The website for Native American Technology and Art http://nativetech. org/. Additional sources are museums for Native American art including The National Museum of the American Indian – Smithsonian Institute http://www. nmai.si.edu. See Appendix 2 for further resources.

Although pinch pots are common in most Native American regions, focusing on settlements along the east coast of the United States, particularly the northeast will turn up the most fruitful results.

Special needs adaptation

This experience does not require any adaptations for children with special needs, though staff should not proceed with this experience until children are able to manipulate clay into a ball.

Shapes and art elements

EXPLORING SHAPES

When

Use this experience only after children have started exploring the possibilities of mark making.

Educators should start with one shape such as a circle. This experience can be repeated with each additional shape. This example uses a circle.

Materials

1 Large white paper.
2 Thick-nib felt tips.

Motivation

1 Look at a chosen shape cutout of sugar paper (see Figure Ex. 7.1). Have an aesthetic experience and encourage children to try to make their bodies into the selected shape. If children are learning about a circle, ask them to make their body round like a ball.
2 Discover the chosen shape in the classroom, look at tabletops, cans, and bowls. Look on our bodies for the given shape, for example, our head is round.
3 Go on a walk and look at the shapes in the environment. Look at the shapes of clouds, houses, trees. Which ones are similar to the shape you are learning about? Compare the shapes to the simple sugar paper shape (see Figure Ex. 7.2).
4 Collect natural objects that resemble the shape you are studying. For example if you are learning about a circle, collect objects such as rocks, round leaves.
5 In the classroom, leave the collected objects out for reference.

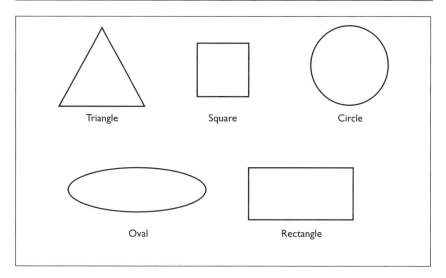

Figure Ex. 7.1   Simple shapes

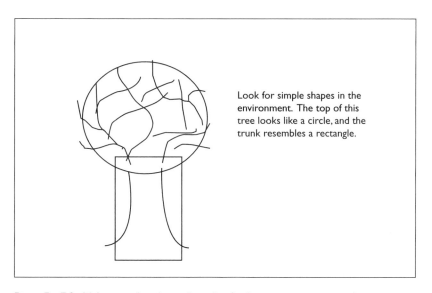

Look for simple shapes in the environment. The top of this tree looks like a circle, and the trunk resembles a rectangle.

Figure Ex. 7.2   Make complex shapes into simple shapes

Art making

This experience is motivation based, however, educators may wish to embark upon an initial shape activity that includes the following:

1 After learning about a new shape, and gathering similarly shaped objects from nature, ask children to observe and study the shape.

2 Have children draw the shape with their finger in the air, in wet sand, in a puddle.

3 Encourage children to draw the shape using a felt tip on large white paper.

4 Ask children now to vary the size of the shape.

5 Look again at the natural objects, model for children observing and trying to draw the shape of the object. Our aim here is not to teach children detailed still life drawing, but to show them how to make connections between objects in nature and their own expressions, how to see, observe, and notice.

Possible discussion or dialogue

1 Using proper terminology, engage children in a dialogue about one chosen shape. Look at, inspect, and discover this shape through all of the senses.

2 If the shape you are exploring is a circle, talk about the idea of round; try to feel round by passing around a ball, or by making your body round. Ask children how they would move if they were round, if they were a circle.

3 When looking for the given shape in the environment, model visual sensitivity, look at parts, not just at whole objects. In other words, if the shape is round, you can look at a bicycle tyre, the dial on a clock, the pupil of an eye.

4 Encourage children to find the same shape in different sizes. Think about why two collected objects of the same shape are different.

5 Look for the given shape in more complex forms. For example, discuss with children where the circular shape can be found on a tree – the leaves? A termite hole? The entire treetop? Refer to Figure Ex. 7.2.

6 When children begin drawing their shape on paper, engage them in dialogue about the process of drawing the shape. Do they have to stretch their arm to reach the top of the shape?

7 If children draw many of the same shape, ask about differences.

8 Educators should listen for dialogue from children that indicates the shape is being used in symbolic representation. For example, 'this circle is the mum', and the like. This type of dialogue opens the doors to infinite possibilities.

FULFILMENT OF THE EARLY LEARNING GOALS FOR CREATIVE DEVELOPMENT

Goal

• Explore colour, texture, shape, form and space in two and three dimensions.

Fulfilment

- Children explore both two- and three-dimensional shapes and forms.

Goal

- Respond in a variety of ways to what they see, hear, smell, touch, and feel.
- Express and communicate their ideas, thoughts and feelings by using a widening range of materials, suitable tools, imaginative and role play, movement, designing and making, and a variety of songs and musical instruments.

Fulfilment

- Children respond both physically and visually to objects discovered in nature.
- Children begin to understand the element of shape as a tool in the formation of their visual expressions.
- Children see both natural and man-made objects as a source of inspiration and as a medium in their visual creations.

Background information and special needs adaptation

There is no background information or special needs adaptations in this experience.

Experience No. 8

Weaving and craft

EXPLORING WEAVING

When

This experience is an initial activity.

Materials

1 Large pieces of square or rectangle-shaped sturdy cardboard (anything over 60 cm is appropriate).
2 Large (big enough to stretch across the pre-cut cardboard) fabric strips of various textures and colours, yarn, twigs, and/or string (use all available materials children could weave with).
3 Masking tape.
4 Photos, reproductions, and any background information (examples of woven items, pictures of woven articles from Africa or Afghanistan; read through experience).

Motivation

1 Bring a number of woven items into the classroom, for example, a jumper, a blanket, a woven mat, a basket. Show the objects to the class; remind them that not all woven objects are flat or soft. Look at the patterns created by the weaving.
2 Take one of the woven objects apart for the children. Show children how the materials interlock. Explore the idea of under and over. Have two children stand up and hold hands. Have a third child walk *under* the connected hands. Next, have two other children sit and hold hands, ask the same child to now walk *over* the connected hands. Let all of the children physically act out the actions under and over.
3 Look at woven fabrics in the dress-up box. Think about how they are different, where they are from.
4 Fabric is not the only material we weave with; think of other materials that can be used in weaving. Go into the natural environment and look for objects to weave

such as twigs, tall grass, branches. Think about objects in the natural environment that are woven or even intertwined, for example, a bird's nest.

5 If the class has already engaged in an initial weaving experience, staff may now wish to introduce the idea of a loom. Furthermore, an encounter with art can include woven objects by African, Afghanistan, or Persian weavers. See Figure Ex. 8.1.

6 Aesthetically explore the textures and colours of the fabrics we are using in our own weavings.

Figure Ex. 8.1 Various woven objects include (clockwise from top left): a basket from China, a Borona milk vessel from Africa, a rug from Afghanistan, the top of a wedding basket from Nigeria

Source: Courtesy collection M. Eglinton, tribalhouse.net.

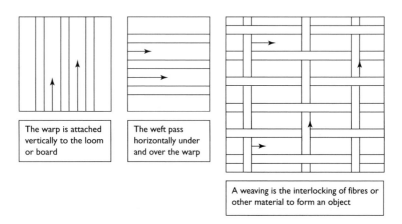

The warp is attached vertically to the loom or board

The weft pass horizontally under and over the warp

A weaving is the interlocking of fibres or other material to form an object

Figure Ex. 8.2 Weaving

Art making

Since this experience is very physical, staff will play an active role in the actual construction of the children's weavings:

1 Educators give each child previously prepared cardboard 'looms'. On each loom staff should have attached the fabric strips that serve as the *warp* (see background information). Educators can attach these fabrics with heavy masking tape on the reverse of the cardboard. Some children may be advanced enough to complete this task on their own.

2 Children choose their own fabric strips and collected natural objects that will become the *weft*. Model for children running the weft over and under the warp. See Figure Ex. 8.2.

3 When the children have completed the weaving, staff should help fasten, again with heavy tape, the ends of the weft onto the reverse of the cardboard. To secure the natural objects that will not bend around the cardboard, staff should use a touch of PVA glue, placed in a hidden area, on the front of the weaving.

Possible discussion or dialogue

1 Discuss and examine woven objects. Ask children if they have ever heard the word weaving or woven. Seek prior knowledge. Discuss how vastly different woven objects can be, from rugs, to baskets, to our everyday clothing. Refer again to Figure Ex. 8.1.

2 While dismantling a woven object describe for children how the object was put together. Talk about parts and wholes. Describe the actions 'over' and 'under'. As children physically act out these actions, provide the narration.

3 Look again at woven objects; discuss the types of fabrics used, the textures, and the colours. Discuss the idea of pattern; look for patterns in the woven objects.

While looking through the dress-up box, encourage children to touch and describe the textiles. Look at objects not made with fabric, such as a basket. Discuss other materials we can weave with.

4 When collecting objects outside, encourage children to talk about why they are choosing a certain twig or branch. Is the branch, twig, blade of grass 'bendy', flexible, soft?

5 During the process, engage children in a dialogue regarding their process. Are they moving the material under or over the vertical warp? Ask children why they are choosing certain fabrics, objects.

6 Respond to the completed creations. Talk to the children about the textures and colours they may have placed next to each other in their weavings. Ask if any of the materials were hard to use. Encourage children to reflect upon their process, and the subsequent visual creation.

FULFILMENT OF THE EARLY LEARNING GOALS FOR CREATIVE DEVELOPMENT

Goal

• Explore colour, texture, shape, form and space in two and three dimensions.

Fulfilment

• When weaving, children explore both two- and three-dimensional art; flat media is being manipulated and given a sense of depth.
• Children explore the texture created by the weaving itself, by the fabrics, and by the chosen natural objects.
• Children look at colour and pattern.

Goal

• Recognise and explore how sounds can be changed, sing simple songs from memory, recognise repeated sounds and sound patterns and match movements to music.

Fulfilment

• Children learn about visual patterns.

Goal

• Use their imagination in art, design, music, dance, imaginative and role play stories.

Fulfilment

- Children explore the different uses for woven objects; imagining, and thinking about the textiles and woven products of other cultures.

Goal

- Respond in a variety of ways to what they see, hear, smell, touch, and feel.
- Express and communicate their ideas, thoughts and feelings by using a widening range of materials, suitable tools, imaginative and role play, movement, designing and making, and a variety of songs and musical instruments.

Fulfilment

- Children respond to the textures of the fabrics, natural objects, and woven goods.
- Children respond, through the formation of visual expression, to the information they gathered through their senses.
- Children use both natural and man-made objects to create woven designs.
- Children use everyday materials in the creation of art.
- Children learn how to use weaving as a potential way to communicate expression.

Background information

Weaving, the interlocking of fabrics or other suitable materials to form an object, is one of the oldest crafts. The warp is the fibres that are attached in a vertical direction to the loom or, in our case, piece of card. The weft is the fibres that pass horizontally over and under the warp.

Special needs adaptations

There are no special needs adaptations for this experience.

Collage and shape

MATISSE COLLAGE

When

This experience is used only after children have explored *all* the different shapes in Shapes and art elements (Experience No. 7), and when children are physically capable of tearing or cutting paper.

Materials

1 Coloured sugar paper.
2 Child's scissors.
3 A3 white card.
4 Glue sticks or small brushes and PVA glue.
5 A collection of natural objects including leaves, flower petals, acorns, and so forth.
6 Photos, reproductions, and any background information (Henri Matisse; read through experience).

Motivation

1 Educators remind children of the different shapes they have already learned about. Look again at circles, ovals, squares, and the like. Also, look at shapes that are not perfect circles, which do not have straight edges. Look around the classroom for 'imperfect' shapes (see Figure Ex. 9.1).
2 Go outside and look again for these imperfect shapes in the environment. Look at the clouds, the treetops, leaves, or a puddle. Collect some of these imperfect shapes (look for oddly shaped leaves, acorns), see Figure Ex. 9.2. Also try to find some objects (can be natural or man-made that are very much like a shape you have already explored such as a circle or a rectangle – look for bricks or well-shaped rocks). Model visual sensitivity and look for shapes in not so obvious places.

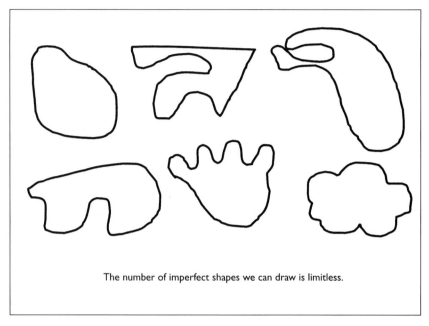

The number of imperfect shapes we can draw is limitless.

Figure Ex. 9.1 Drawn imperfect shapes

3 Bring the natural objects inside for further exploration. Engage in an aesthetic experience, encourage children to feel the form of the objects with both hands, to really look at the shape. Staff might ask children to try to draw the shape of the object.

4 Introduce children to the work of artist Henri Matisse. Encounter art and show children reproductions of his famous 'cut-outs' or collages. Compare some of the shapes in his cut-outs to the shapes of the objects we gathered in nature.

5 Leave the Matisse reproductions out for children to get to know, explore, and discover.

6 Think about collage, the process of collage. Ask children how they think Matisse created the chosen pictures. Have a real collage in the room available for children to touch and examine (staff can make their own simple collages out of sturdy paper on card). Model the collage process.

Art making

1 After a thorough look at the work of Matisse, children will make their own collages.

2 Have children select a few of the natural objects they have been exploring. Ask children to try to replicate the shape of the object in paper. They can cut or tear the shape out. Use Matisse's collages as inspiration.

Figure Ex. 9.2   There are many different shapes in the environment. Look for new and
unusual shapes, shapes with soft edges, out of the ordinary and interesting
shapes

Source: Photo by M. Eglinton.

3 When children have cut or torn a few shapes, use the process of collage to
arrange them on the card. Children can use glue sticks or PVA glue and a brush to
adhere the shapes to the card.

4 Encourage proper clean-up of the collage materials.

Possible discussion or dialogue

1 Remind children of the shapes they have already learned. Discuss how these
shapes are different from less 'perfect' shapes such as clouds or other objects with
soft or uneven edges.

2 Talk about a variety of shapes, such as the shape of a pear, a leaf, an ear of corn.
Compare these shapes with the shapes children have previously been studying.

3 When outside, engage children in dialogue about the shapes in nature, how they
are different from the perfect cut-out ones we have been looking at in the class.
Bring some of these perfect cut shapes outside with you to show the children.
Compare the straight edges of the sugar paper cut-out to the fuzzy edges or irregular
shape of a leaf or other natural object.

4 When the objects from nature are collected and brought into the classroom,
encourage sensory exploration of the objects. Feel and look at the edges of the

objects, the forms, think about what the objects are used for. Discuss the children's discoveries – prompt them to investigate.

5 When introducing the work of Matisse, initially talk about the shapes. Ask if any of the shapes in the shown works are similar to the natural shapes found outside, or if they are like any of the shapes we have previously learned about. Discuss how shapes are different from each other. Talk also about the colours Matisse uses.

6 Educators will also want to talk about Matisse as an artist, though this information can easily be worked into dialogue throughout the experience.

7 During the art making, talk to children about the objects they choose. Discuss again the properties of the object, the shape and form.

8 Encourage children to talk about the process of collage. How does the glue feel? Are they able to use the scissors? Do they get a better shape if they tear it? Why are they placing one shape in one corner all by itself? Are they thinking about colour?

9 Throughout art making dialogue refer back to Matisse's works.

10 Finally, reflect on the process and respond to the visual works. Talk about colours used, any patterns formed, the medium employed. Look at the natural shapes and compare them to the cut-out or torn shapes.

FULFILMENT OF THE EARLY LEARNING GOALS FOR CREATIVE DEVELOPMENT

Goal

- Explore colour, texture, shape, form and space in two and three dimensions.

Fulfilment

- By touching forms and creating two-dimensional shapes, children discover shape and form.
- Through the work of Matisse and the creation of their own collages, children explore colour.
- Children understand space when shapes begin to fill the paper.
- Children study forms in the environment.

Goal

- Recognise and explore how sounds can be changed, sing simple songs from memory, recognise repeated sounds and sound patterns and match movements to music.

Fulfilment

- Children discover visual patterns and repeated shapes.

Goal

- Respond in a variety of ways to what they see, hear, smell, touch, and feel.
- Express and communicate their ideas, thoughts and feelings by using a widening range of materials, suitable tools, imaginative and role play, movement, designing and making, and a variety of songs and musical instruments.

Fulfilment

- Children respond to shape and form by exploring it through the senses.
- Children discuss the media employed, and respond to natural/man-made objects.
- Children begin to understand how to communicate ideas through the process of collage.
- Children look to both nature and art history for inspiration.

Background information

Henri Matisse (1869–1954), perhaps one of the most important French artists of the twentieth century, began making collages when his failing health confined him to a wheelchair. Before this, Matisse was best known for his paintings. When deciding which Matisse collages to show the children, educators have a vast selection; narrow the choices down by finding collages with somewhat simple natural shapes and bright bold colours – the less complex the better. Note, Matisse made many of his collages in the late 1940s and early 1950s.

Reproductions and further information on Matisse can be referenced in twentieth-century art history books, or encyclopedias and CD-ROMs (see Appendix 2 for resources). The artist's brief biography, examples of his work, and links to related sites can be found on the Artcyclopedia website: http://www. artcyclopedia.com.

Special needs adaptation

Special needs children may need to use adapted scissors.

Clay and craft 2

CLAY TILES

When

Use this lesson after children have successfully completed Initial clay experience (Experience No. 1).

Materials

1 Air-dry or natural clay.
2 Cardboard material to rest clay on.
3 Small bowls with water.
4 Selection of wooden clay tools (can use wooden spoons, forks, and tongue depressors), toothpicks.
5 A selection of natural materials (rocks, leaves, twigs, bark) or if in an urban environment use textures found in the classroom such as corrugated cardboard or objects found in the urban environment such as wire, rope, or netting.
6 Mixture of PVA glue and water (ratio one-part glue/three-parts water), and brushes to apply the mixture.
7 Rolling pin (if one is not available, use a cardboard tube or plastic bottle).
8 Photos, reproductions, and any background information (clay tiles from various parts of the world; read through experience).

Motivation

1 Show children the clay, remind children of what they learned about clay in their initial clay explorations.
2 Introduce children to ceramic tiles. Encounter art and inspire children by showing them pictures of tiles from England, the Middle East, Europe, North Africa, or Mexico. Look at the colours, shapes, textures, markings. If possible, try to bring in a real Islamic, Mexican, or European tile. Leave this tile out for close inspection. Look at and try to draw some of the designs. See Figure Ex. 10.1.

Figure Ex. 10.1   A beautiful clay tile from Morocco
Source: Courtesy collection M. Eglinton, tribalhouse.net.

3 Look around the classroom and try to find tiles in your own environment.
4 Go for a walk and look for tiles.
5 On your walk to discover tiles, look also for natural objects that inspire, leave an impression, or have an interesting texture; gather the object for art making.
6 Use the media as a motivator, allow children ample time before forming their tiles to pound, explore, and reacquaint themselves with clay.

Art making

1 Give children time to discover the clay again. Encourage sensory exploration.
2 After this initial exploration, ask children to take a chunk of clay (approximately twice the size of their fist), and flatten it first with their fists and then with the rolling pin.
3 When clay is suitably flattened (approximately 2 cm) the educator, with the help of the child, should cut the clay into a tile shape using a toothpick or wooden tongue depressor.
4 Place the tile on a piece of cardboard.
5 Encourage children to use the natural objects to create a textured pattern or simple marks on the surface of the tile.
6 When the tiles are finished, staff, again with the help of children, cover the tile with the PVA glue and water mixture.

Possible discussion or dialogue

1 With any clay experience staff should always encourage children to talk about the properties of clay – how does it feel, look, smell?

2 Talk about the uses of clay. How it is used in everyday life. Think about all of the places you find tiles (bathroom, kitchen, floor).

3 Discuss tiles from other cultures. How are they similar, different? Talk about the colours, the patterns, designs. Talk about the uses of tiles in other cultures. How are the Islamic tiles different from the tiles on our kitchen floor?

4 On your walk outside look for tiles on walls, on houses, again discuss the uses of tiles. See Figure Ex. 10.2.

5 While looking for textured objects to decorate your tiles with, encourage children to talk about the objects they may be looking for, or ask children why they are drawn to certain textures. Ask them to imagine how certain textures will look pressed into the clay.

6 When making the tile, engage children in a dialogue regarding the process. How hard do they have to pound the clay to flatten it? Is the rolling pin hard to use? How do they want their tile shaped? Is it easy to push the texture into the clay? Are they getting the design or pattern they want?

7 Continue discussing the tiles children encountered. Leave out the various sample tiles or tile pictures for dialogue throughout the process.

Figure Ex. 10.2 Look for tiles in the constructed environment. Here, hand-made tiles grace the outdoor children's play area at *Kids Unlimited* St Mary's nursery in Hulme, Manchester

Source: Photo by M. Eglinton.

8 Discuss proper care for the art materials.

9 Reflect and respond to the finished tiles. Look again at the tiles from other countries. Talk about the difference between the children's tiles and, say, tiles from North Africa. Encourage children to talk about what they would use their tiles for. Ask children what they would like to do next with clay.

10 If you have not already, begin to talk about how clay hardens, how clay needs to be cooked in an oven called a kiln or, how in some places, it is baked in a fire.

FULFILMENT OF THE EARLY LEARNING GOALS FOR CREATIVE DEVELOPMENT

Goal

•   Explore colour, texture, shape, form and space in two and three dimensions.

Fulfilment

•   Children explore the properties of clay through the senses.
•   Children discover texture when they use objects to decorate their clay tiles.
•   Children shape and form their tiles; they explore form and shape in both two and three dimensions.
•   Children transform a malleable three-dimensional material into two-dimensions.

Goal

•   Use their imagination in art and design, music, dance, imaginative and role play and stories.

Fulfilment

•   Children explore the clay tiles of other cultures.
•   Children imagine life in other cultures; they compare our tiles with the tiles of various cultures.
•   Children think about uses for their tiles.
•   Children imagine their one tile as part of a wall of tiles – as a piece of the environment.

Goal

•   Respond in a variety of ways to what they see, hear, smell, touch, and feel.
•   Express and communicate their ideas, thoughts and feelings by using a widening range of materials, suitable tools, imaginative and role play, movement, designing and making, and a variety of songs and musical instruments.

Fulfilment

- Children respond to the clay by exploring it through the senses.
- Children discuss the texture created by the natural/man-made objects.
- Children use art media to create both an artistic and useful object.
- Children begin to explore the use of natural objects in the formation of expression.
- Children design both functional and non-functional art.
- Children are introduced to new tools, such as the rolling pin.

Background information

Many cultures and countries produce incredible, inspiring tiles. Tiles from around the world can be found in most world ceramics and specialist tile books. Two such books are R.J. Charleston (ed.), *World Ceramics*, London: Hamlyn (1968); and N. Riley, *Tile Art: A History of Decorative Ceramic Tiles*, London: Quintet (1987).

There are a number of websites with information and pictures of tiles including The Encyclopedia Smithsonian http://www.si.edu/resource/faq/, click on ceramics and find the link to Ceramic Tiles and Architectural Terra Cotta. This link features a full bibliography of tile books. Also, see Tiles on the Web http://www.tiles.org/.

Special needs adaptation

Children with special physical needs may require assistance flattening and rolling out the clay, and cutting the tile.

Colour and art elements 1

EXPLORING COLOUR

When

This experience is an initial exploratory lesson; however, it is best to offer it after children have already completed Initial painting experience (Experience No. 2), as the art making section in this experience involves the children in paint mixing.

Educators should start with one colour, in this example, we use the colour blue. Repeat with each additional colour.

Materials

1 Finger paint or thick school paint (blue, white, and black).
2 Large white paper.
3 Various brushes.
4 Paint pots.
5 Bowls of water.
6 Photos, reproductions, and any background information (Pablo Picasso; read through experience).

Motivation

1 Bring a variety of blue materials to the classroom, for example, blue painted objects such as picture frames, blue plastic cups, blue beads, blue fabrics and fibres, blue sugar paper, etc. Look at all the blue objects. Look around the classroom for other blue objects or for the colour blue. Look at all the different shades or types of blue. Some are very light and others are dark.
2 Have an aesthetic experience: go into the environment and look for the colour blue. Find natural blues, such as the blue of the sky, and man-made blues, for instance, the blue paint on a house.
3 Encounter art by introducing a reproduction of a painting from Pablo Picasso's Blue Period. Study the *shades* of blue, try to count how many different kinds of

blue are in one painting. Note, educators exploring other colours should look for works by artists that use predominantly your chosen colour of study – a good look though any art history book will turn up a multitude of examples.

4 Leave all blue objects and Picasso reproductions out for further investigation.

Art making

This experience is motivation based, however, educators may still wish to embark on simple art making experiences:

1 After learning about the new colour, give children the opportunity to use the colour in their visual expressions.

2 Look again at the various blue objects and at the Picasso paintings. Think about making many types of blue.

3 Give each child a small cup of blue paint. Using a brush or their finger, encourage children to put some of the paint on a piece of paper.

4 Put a small drop of white paint in each child's cup, ask children to mix the paint with a brush, paint the new colour onto the same paper. Continue mixing various shades of blue (by adding drops of white or black to the blue paint); use the given objects and the Picasso painting as inspiration. Make paint mixing into an aesthetic experience.

Possible discussion or dialogue

1 Talk to children about colour. What is it? Where do we find it? What colours do we know?

2 When looking at the blue objects, ask children if every blue colour is the same. Hold two very different blues next to each other and ask 'Is this the same colour?' Talk about blues you can 'see through' such as blue glass, ask children if they can find all of the blue objects in the room. Discuss 'light' blue and 'dark' blue.

3 Before going on a walk, ask children what is blue outside. Is the sky blue? Is the grass blue? When outside, model for children finding blue in not so obvious places, for example, you may find a drop of blue paint on the pavement. Discuss how that drop may have got there. Talk about how blues in nature, such as the sky, are different from man-made blues such as the blue paint on a house.

4 Discuss Picasso's painting. Talk about all the blues he used. Look at and mention how he painted someone's face, hands, or the like in blue. If children seem developmentally ready, ask them how the picture makes them feel. Happy? Sad or blue? Touch on the emotions colours can evoke. Ask 'What colour would you be if you were sad?' Ask 'What does the colour blue make you feel like?' Give children choices, for example, ask 'Does it make you feel cold? Sad? Happy?' Note, there are no wrong answers; our aim is to make children think about colour.

5 Talk about all of the blues in the painting. Count, discuss, and compare them to both each other and to other blue objects in the room.

6 During art making, engage in dialogue with children about the process. How does the blue look on the paper? How does the paint feel? What happens when the white is mixed in with the blue? How does the new colour look on the paper? How does it compare with the old blue? How did we get this new colour? Do any of the blues we have made look like any of the blues in the painting? Are any similar to the blues of the objects?

7 Respond to the final works. Count all of the blues children were able to mix. Reflect on the process. Discuss what they can paint next using the colour blue.

FULFILMENT OF THE EARLY LEARNING GOALS FOR CREATIVE DEVELOPMENT

Goal

• Explore colour, texture, shape, form and space in two and three dimensions.

Fulfilment

• Children explore colour in the environment, in painting, and on three-dimensional objects.
• Children learn about colour by mixing paint.
• Children explore the work of Picasso.

Goal

• Use their imagination in art and design, music, dance, imaginative and role play and stories.

Fulfilment

• Children learn about the imaginative use of colour in the work of Picasso.

Goal

• Respond in a variety of ways to what they see, hear, smell, touch, and feel.
• Express and communicate their ideas, thoughts and feelings by using a widening range of materials, suitable tools, imaginative and role play, movement, designing and making, and a variety of songs and musical instruments.

Fulfilment

• Children feel, see, and essentially touch colour.

- Children connect emotions to colours; they begin to think about colours as causing feelings or emotions.
- Children compare and contrast shades of colour.
- Children actively seek out colour in the environment.
- Children see colour as a tool to use in their creations.
- Children respond and reflect on their processes.
- Children see variety in one colour, and learn that colour mixing will give them this variety.

Background information

Pablo Picasso (1881–1973) was one of the most inventive and prolific artists of the twentieth century. His Blue Period (1901–04) is characterised by paintings created with, for the most part, shades of blue. Examples of Blue Period paintings are easily accessed in art history books and on the Internet (see Appendix 2 for resources). One website that contains information and links to Blue Period paintings is The Artchive http://www.artchive.com, click on the link for Picasso and on Blue Period. Two good examples of Blue Period paintings educators may want to use are *The Old Guitarist*, 1903, The Art Institute of Chicago or *Woman and Child by the Sea*, 1902, private collection, Japan.

Special needs adaptations

There are no special needs adaptations for this experience, though educators will want to make sure children are almost able to hold a paintbrush before beginning.

Mark making

MARKS AND MUSIC

When

Use this experience only after children have already begun exploring the possibilities of drawing, shapes, colours, and are able to handle drawing media. This experience can be repeated using colours or shapes. Here the lesson features marks.

Materials

1 Large white paper (three sheets per child).
2 Thick-nib felt tips.
3 Three different types of music, for example, jazz, classical, pop.
4 A stereo to play music on.

Motivation

1 Take time to listen to each piece of music. Get children acquainted with each musical work over a period of days (or weeks). Feel each selection, encourage children to hear the music. Physically respond to the music through dance. Make listening to music an aesthetic experience.
2 Listen for patterns in the musical selections, try to envision colours, lines, and shapes within the music. Listen for speed within the music.
3 Listen for differences between the pieces of music.
4 Model for children making marks to a piece of music (do not use one of the pieces children have been studying, but use a different piece in the same genre). Draw quick marks or long fluid line depending on your response to the music at the particular time. For example, a piece of classical music may feature moments of staccato or disconnected notes in which case you may make quick marks across the paper, and moments where the notes are very melodious, flowing almost endlessly. This could be reflected using long lines drawn from one side of the paper to the other. See Figure Ex. 12.1.

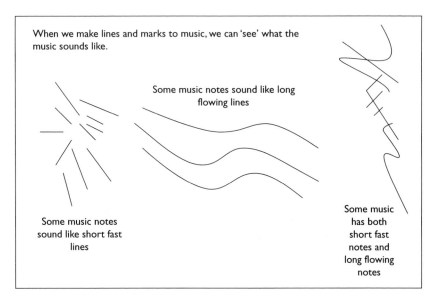

When we make lines and marks to music, we can 'see' what the music sounds like.

Some music notes sound like long flowing lines

Some music notes sound like short fast lines

Some music has both short fast notes and long flowing notes

Figure Ex. 12.1 Making marks to music

5 When children have a general understanding of the connection between visual works and music, let them begin their own visual responses to music.

Art making

1 Give each child one large piece of white paper and let them choose a large felt tip of their choice.
2 Play the first selection of music, encourage children to respond physically and to 'chart' the music visually.
3 Do the same for each piece of music. Use a different sheet of paper and let children select a coloured felt tip of their choice for each musical and visual composition.

Possible discussion or dialogue

1 After listening to a piece of music, encourage children to react physically to the music, ask them to dance, run, and move to the music. Talk about what the music reminds them of, how it makes them feel. Is it happy music? Does it remind them, for example, of the beach? Listen and respond to parts of the same piece of music. Ask children about differences within the music.
2 Talk about what types of lines children imagine in the music, listen for individual notes, what would a line look like that sounded like that note?; model for children what you think the line would look like.

3 After spending time with all three pieces of music, talk about the differences and similarities between all three pieces. In addition, educators may wish to re-inforce learning about differences and similarities by asking children to compare and contrast three very different visual marks.

4 When staff model their own visual responses to the music, they should talk clearly about their thoughts and process. For example, as a piece of music increases tempo, an educator may want to reveal 'my felt tip is running with the music' or, if the music is soft, 'my line feels so sleepy', reflect this 'sleep' with a light line and point out 'my line is so tired it can barely press down on the paper'.

5 When children begin to respond to the music, talk to them about why they have chosen a certain coloured felt tip, how the music feels, what their processes are.

6 When all three works are completed, display them and listen to the music again. Talk about similarities and differences between the pieces. Think about other noises you can draw – a bird's song, the buzzing of a bee?

7 Reflect on the processes used; discuss other visual ways we could respond to music – with shapes? Colours? Paint? Clay models? What about textures?

FULFILMENT OF THE EARLY LEARNING GOALS FOR CREATIVE DEVELOPMENT

Goal

• Explore colour, texture, shape, form and space in two and three dimensions.

Fulfilment

• Children choose colours and lines to suit their visual needs.
• Children see the differences and similarities between created marks.

Goal

• Recognise and explore how sounds can be changed, sing simple songs from memory, recognise repeated sounds and sound patterns and match movements to music.

Fulfilment

• Children discover musical patterns.
• Children seek out repeated rhythms.
• Children relate sound to vision.
• Children relate body movements to sound.
• Children connect sound patterns with visual patterns.

Goal

- Use their imagination in art and design, music, dance, imaginative and role play and stories.

Fulfilment

- Children think about sequencing in music and in art.
- Children imagine the relationship between music and art.
- Children see their drawing medium as a character mapping out the music, responding to sound.

Goal

- Respond in a variety of ways to what they see, hear, smell, touch, and feel.
- Express and communicate their ideas, thoughts and feelings by using a widening range of materials, suitable tools, imaginative and role play, movement, designing and making, and a variety of songs and musical instruments.

Fulfilment

- Children relate music to visual communication.
- Children use marks to respond to sound, and to communicate visual associations.
- Children engage in a multi-sensory experience.
- Children hear a variety of musical types.

Background information

Visual artists and musicians have long appreciated the relationship between art and music. Many artists respond visually to music, many musicians use the visual arts as a source of inspiration. Throughout this experience try to employ words common to both disciplines such as harmony and unity, piece, work or composition, pattern and repetition, mood and feeling, refer to notes as marks and marks as notes.

Special needs adaptations

Children with hearing impairments will need special attention during this experience. For children with hearing difficulties put particular emphasis on 'seeing' and 'feeling' the music rather than on listening and hearing.

Textiles and craft

TIE DYEING

When

This experience is an initial activity.

Materials

1 White cotton cloth (cut into squares), or small white cotton tee shirts.
2 Rubber bands.
3 Natural objects (stones, acorns, etc.).
4 Sieve.
5 Large bowl half filled with water and a pinch of salt.
6 For the dye educators can use strained and mashed *edible* berries (frozen or picked), dark coloured fruit juice such as cranberry or grape, or cold tea.

Motivation

1 Show children different coloured fabrics and textiles.
2 Think about how fabrics get their colour. Try to figure out what objects in nature are the same colour as the fabric you are discussing. For example, if the fabric you hold up is green, think about the grass or leaves.
3 Encounter art; think about how people 'dyed' their clothes before we had machines and man-made dye. Have some natural materials available; show children how colour can be extracted from natural objects. For example, rub some grass along a white piece of fabric, see the green trail it leaves, or pound a fallen dandelion between two pieces of cloth, open the cloth up and show children the colourful results.
4 Introduce children to tie dyeing. Do not show examples, but tell children it is a way of making 'patterns' and 'designs' on cloth.
5 Continue inspiring children by using the sieve and perhaps a masher to extract the juice from the berries; catch the liquid in the bowl filled halfway with water

and a pinch of salt. Smell, touch, taste (make sure children do not have any allergies to the materials before allowing tasting), look at, and listen to the liquid being strained or poured; make it an aesthetic experience.

Art making

1 After deciding on the colours and material, you will be dyeing the cloth with, model for children wrapping a natural object in part of the cloth and securing with a rubber band. (Note, the use of a natural object wrapped in the cloth is optional, it only has a slight impact on the finished design.)

2 Encourage children to do the same. Wrap at least three sections of the cloth. Staff should support children with this step, ensuring that the rubber bands are very tight (the idea is the rubber bands resist the coloured liquid, the result is the tie dyed design).

3 Have each child place their rubber-banded cloth into the liquid (staff may want to have a number of dyeing bowls available, perhaps with two different colouring choices, for example, one with tea and the other with berry or grape juice).

4 Give each child a chance to gently agitate the liquid, ensuring full coverage of the cloth.

5 Let the materials soak for at least one hour.

6 Remove the cloth from the liquid, wring it out, and allow drying until damp. When damp, remove the rubber bands and air dry.

Possible discussion or dialogue

1 Discuss a variety of fabrics, the texture, colours, and patterns.

2 Talk about colouring techniques, machines, dye. Ask children how they think fabrics get their colour; seek prior knowledge. Encourage children to connect the colours of the fabric with the colours in the natural environment.

3 Ask children how they think people dyed their clothes before we had machines. Imagine there were no stores to buy coloured clothing, ask children how they could make their clothes coloured. Connect this thought to the colours found in natural materials. Show children what happens when we rub grass on cloth. Ask how the cloth got that new green streak. Where did the green come from? What else can we extract colour from?

4 Talk about how some fabrics have patterns and designs on them, encourage children to articulate how these patterns or designs are made.

5 Discuss tie dyeing as a way of getting patterns.

6 Engage in dialogue about the natural dye we are employing. What does it smell, look, taste, and sound like?

7 Talk about the process of tying and securing the rubber band, how the fabric looks when it begins to soak in the natural colour, ask children what they think the cloth will look like when it comes out. Will it look the same as before? What will change? Will it look, smell, taste different? Will it have patterns? Designs? How? Where will these designs come from?

8 Discuss the process of removing the rubber bands. Is it harder to take them off or put them on? What does the fabric look like underneath? Is it different to the rest of the fabric?

9 Respond to the final works. How is the fabric altered? Does it smell, feel, look different than it did before we dyed it? Can we see any patterns? Designs? Look for similarities and differences between all the children's works. Reflect on the process, and encourage children to think of ways to use their new fabrics – in a role play? In the environment? To wear?

FULFILMENT OF THE EARLY LEARNING GOALS FOR CREATIVE DEVELOPMENT

Goal

•   Explore colour, texture, shape, form and space in two and three dimensions.

Fulfilment

•   Children learn the means by which materials are coloured.
•   Children explore the textures of fabrics.
•   Children taste, smell, feel, and listen to colours.
•   Children learn colour can be extracted from a variety of materials, including natural and man-made objects.

Goal

•   Recognise and explore how sounds can be changed, sing simple songs from memory, recognise repeated sounds and sound patterns and match movements to music.

Fulfilment

•   Children learn about and look for visual patterns.

Goal

•   Use their imagination in art, design, music, dance, imaginative and role play stories.

Fulfilment

•   Children explore primitive dyeing techniques.
•   Children learn sequencing.

- Children think about using their creations in role play.
- Children imagine life before machines and modern conveniences.

Goal

- Respond in a variety of ways to what they see, hear, smell, touch, and feel.
- Express and communicate their ideas, thoughts and feelings by using a widening range of materials, suitable tools, imaginative and role play, movement, designing and making, and a variety of songs and musical instruments.

Fulfilment

- Children discover colour through all of the senses.
- Children learn colour extracted from nature has a smell and a taste.
- Children use both man-made and natural objects to create both functional and non-functional art.
- Children learn nature provides with an abundance of artistic materials.
- Children understand the use of fabric and textiles in art.

Background information

Tie dyeing is a way of getting a pattern on fabric by tying, knotting, or sealing off areas of the fabric from the liquid dye. Tie dyeing works by resisting the dye in certain places to form the pattern or design. Tie dyeing, wildly popular in the 1960s, is still used by textile artists and clothing designers today.

Special needs adaptations

There are no special needs adaptations for this experience.

Painting and art elements

GEORGIA O'KEEFFE FLOWERS

When

Use this experience after children have finished initial exploratory experiences in two-dimensional art including Initial painting experience (Experience No. 2), Shapes and art elements (Experience No. 7), and Colour and art elements 1 (Experience No. 11). For less advanced children, place emphasis on discovery and motivation.

Materials

1 Large white paper.
2 Dripless paint such as finger paint or thick school paint in blue, green, red, yellow, white, and black.
3 Brushes.
4 Pencils.
5 Felt tips.
6 Assorted flowers – try to use flowers with simple design such as daisies, buttercups, and the like.
7 Mixing bowls for the paint.
8 Bowls of water.
9 Photos, reproductions, and any background information (Georgia O'Keeffe; read through experience).

Motivation

1 Encounter art; introduce the work of artist Georgia O'Keeffe, show children a variety of her various flower paintings.
2 Look at real flowers and compare them to the work of O'Keeffe.
3 Look at the real flowers under a magnifying glass; again compare the flower to the flowers in O'Keeffe's paintings.

Figure Ex. 14.1 Looking closely at a flower opens up numerous artistic possibilities
Source: Photo by M. Eglinton.

4 Discover just one part of the flower, encourage children to look at one section – a petal, the pistil (generally the centre of the flower), the small leaves underneath the flower top.

5 Engage in aesthetic experience, using a magnifying glass or a microscope discover nuance within the flower parts. See Figure Ex. 14.1.

6 Look for designs, patterns, and colour variations.

7 Have further aesthetic experiences by taking your magnifying glasses outside and find patterns, designs, gradations in tree bark, grass, the dirt.

8 Back inside look again at O'Keeffe's paintings, this time exploring the shapes she uses, the various colours. Look for a simple design in her work.

9 Think about O'Keeffe's work, what was she trying to do? How do the paintings make us feel?

Art making

1 Using O'Keeffe's work as inspiration, encourage children to look again at one section of a real flower under a magnifying glass.

2 Ask children to simplify the flower and look only for the shapes, the edges, or any designs made by distinct lines. See Figure Ex. 14.2.

3 Have children draw the observed lines, shapes, or design on white paper using a pencil; encourage children to draw the design or shapes very large, remind them

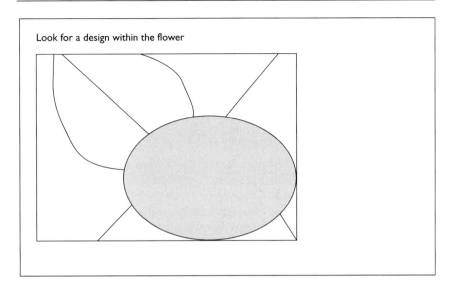

Look for a design within the flower

Figure Ex. 14.2 Design in nature

of O'Keeffe's paintings. Note, some children will choose to draw the whole flower, if that is the case, encourage them to draw it as large as possible to highlight the flower's natural design.

4 When children have completed their design, ask them to go over the lines they have made with a darker medium – this could be a thick felt tip, black paint, or a thick black crayon.

5 Have children look at the colour of their flower part, ask them what colour they would like to use to paint their design. (Note, we only ask children to look again at the colour of their flower to exercise their visual sensitivity, not so they can copy the colour.) Children can paint their design any colour they wish.

6 As children paint their compositions, alert them to the different parts of the design. Ask them if they want to keep it all one colour or if they wish to vary the colours. Enable them to employ the media by helping them mix the colours they want to use.

Possible discussion or dialogue

1 Engage children in a dialogue about the work of Georgia O'Keeffe. While showing reproductions of her paintings, ask children if they can guess what the paintings are. What do they look like? Are they just patterns and designs? Are they objects? Is it a person? A tree?

2 Compare real flowers to O'Keeffe's paintings, look for the similarities, the differences, and compare colours, shapes, designs, and patterns.

3 When looking at the real flowers under a magnifying glass, talk to children about

the designs in the flower, ask them if they see shapes, ask how the real flower up-close compares with Georgia O'Keeffe's flowers.

4 Use proper terminology when referring to parts of the flower.

5 When discovering one part of the flower, encourage children to describe what they see. What colour is it? What shape? How is it different from the rest of the flower?

6 When outside, model talking about the nuances you see when you study an object from nature under a magnifying glass. For example, while looking at tree bark you may reveal, 'I thought it was only brown, but now I see different types of brown colours and some reds too. The bumps form a design. I can see dark lines running through it.' Encourage children to do the same with grass, leaves, flowers, rocks.

7 Discuss O'Keeffe as an artist. Tell children where she lived, how she collected and made paintings of bones and other natural objects she found in the desert.

8 Look at her paintings again, discuss how they make children feel, are they happy? Do they remind us of anything? Do you want to reach out and touch them? Smell them?

9 When children work, encourage them to observe and refer to the real flower as much as possible. Ask them what part they are looking at, how they would like to draw it; ask if they can see shapes.

10 Engage in dialogue with children throughout the process. Are they having trouble mixing the paint? Drawing the observed shapes?

11 Respond verbally to the final visual outcomes, talk about the colours children were able to mix, the designs they made, the shapes they found. Have children reflect on their artistic processes. Link a future experience by asking, 'What other objects in nature might look different under the magnifying glass?'

FULFILMENT OF THE EARLY LEARNING GOALS FOR CREATIVE DEVELOPMENT

Goal

- Explore colour, texture, shape, form and space in two and three dimensions.

Fulfilment

- By touching and discovering the form in flowers, and by creating two-dimensional designs, children discover shape and form.
- Children explore colour, form and space, and shape in the paintings of artist Georgia O'Keeffe.
- Children discover colour, texture, and form in the environment.
- Children learn about colour through mixing the paint, and applying colour to their creations.
- Children think about space when they enlarge part of an object onto the surface of the paper.

Goal

- Recognise and explore how sounds can be changed, sing simple songs from memory, recognise repeated sounds and sound patterns and match movements to music.

Fulfilment

- Children discover visual patterns and repeated shapes.

Goal

- Respond in a variety of ways to what they see, hear, smell, touch, and feel.
- Express and communicate their ideas, thoughts and feelings by using a widening range of materials, suitable tools, imaginative and role play, movement, designing and making, and a variety of songs and musical instruments.

Fulfilment

- Children respond to objects in the environment through sensory exploration, observation, and visual representation.
- Children look at and talk about the work of artist Georgia O'Keeffe.
- Children discuss the media employed, and respond to natural/man-made objects.
- Children make the connection between the natural environment and their own visual outpourings.
- Children learn the importance of 'looking closely', discovering, and scrutinising an object or material.
- Children will begin to understand how to communicate ideas through the process of drawing and painting.
- Children will look to both nature and art history for inspiration.
- Children learn how to make colours by mixing them together.

Background information

Georgia O'Keeffe (1887–1986) is one of the most celebrated American painters of the twentieth century. Her enlarged abstract flowers, skulls, and bone studies are among some of her most well-known pieces. When choosing a reproduction to show the children, seek one with a bold design of a truly abstract nature such as *Jack-in-the-Pulpit IV* (1930) from the collection of Georgia O'Keeffe. Reproductions and further information on O'Keeffe can be referenced in most twentieth-century art history books, or encyclopedias and CD-ROMs (see Appendix 4 for resources). The artist's brief biography, examples of her work, and

links to related sites can be found on the Artcyclopedia website: http://www.
artcyclopedia.com.

Special needs adaptation

There are no special needs adaptations, though educators should be keenly aware
of children's artistic development before engaging them in this advanced art
experience.

Clay

CLAY MODELS

When

This is an advanced clay experience; use only after children have successfully finished the other three clay lessons including Initial clay experience (Experience No. 1), pinch pots, Clay and craft 1 (Experience No. 6), and tiles, Clay and craft 2 (Experience No. 10).

Materials

1 Air-dry or natural clay.
2 Cardboard material to rest clay on.
3 Small bowls with water.
4 Selection of wooden clay tools (can use wooden spoons, forks, and tongue depressors).
5 Broken up toothpicks.
6 Mixture of PVA glue and water (ratio one-part glue/three-parts water), and brushes to apply the mixture.
7 Photos, reproductions, and any background information (Meso-American, Olmec ceramics; read through experience).

Note, this experience uses Olmec ceramics for inspiration; however, educators can choose any Meso-American ceramics (or, indeed, ceramics from another area of the world) to encounter. Whatever educators choose, be sure the ceramics shown are models and figurines, not vessels.

Motivation

1 Show children the clay, remind children of what they learned about clay in previous clay experiences.
2 Think about other objects made out of clay. Encounter art; show children pictures

Figure Ex. 15.1 Olmec ceramic figures
Source: Courtesy collection M. Eglinton, tribalhouse.net.

of Olmec ceramics. Look at the shapes, the forms, the surface of the clay. Think about what life was like when these forms were created. See Figure Ex. 15.1.
3 Think about how to make clay models. What would you need? What would you make? Would it be an animal? A person? Or maybe just a shape? Ask the more advanced children to draw a picture of what they would like to make in clay.

Art making

1 Give children time to discover the clay again. Encourage sensory exploration.
2 After this initial exploration, ask children to think again about the Olmec or Meso-American ceramics, bring the pictures out for inspiration. Remind children of how they made the pinch pots.
3 Ask children to make two small pinch pots. Help children attach the two pinch pots together to form a large oval or circular form. This is the body or main part of the model.
4 Encourage children to fashion other parts of the model from the left-over clay. Adults will now need to help children attach the parts to the main section of the model. Clay parts can be attached using small pieces of broken toothpicks. Put part of the toothpick into the piece of clay to be attached, and then push the part into the main body of the model. See Figure Ex. 15.2.
5 Add textures and markings to the finished model using left-over pieces of toothpick and the wooden clay tools.

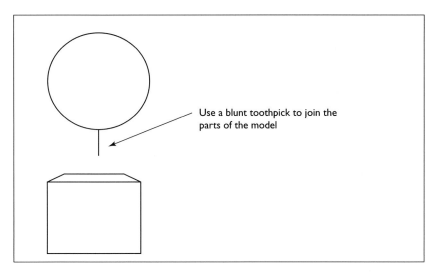

Figure Ex. 15.2 Model construction

6 With the help of adults, cover the entire model with a PVA glue and water mixture.

Possible discussion or dialogue

1 In the beginning of any clay lesson children should engage in a dialogue about the properties of clay. Build on the children's prior knowledge and discover their learning so far.

2 Talk to the children about their pinch pots; ask if they can think of other objects made out of clay. Introduce clay models by showing children pictures of Olmec or Meso-American ceramic figurines.

3 Prompt children to discover the ceramic figurines, to think about the formed object, what it may have been used for, how it was made, why it looks different from our pinch pots or ceramic tiles. Support children's ideas regarding how they think the forms were made, tools used, uses of the forms.

4 Engage in a dialogue about Olmec life, the Olmec artist who made the forms.

5 During art making, ask children to describe the clay. How does it feel? Smell? Look? How does it look different to the Olmec forms?

6 Talk again about the pinch pots. Do children remember how they made them? Can anyone describe the steps? When children begin, help them describe the process involved.

7 Discuss the forms the children are thinking about. What parts do they require? Are they making a shape? An animal? A person? Promote dialogue about the fashioning of parts for the models. Get children to think about parts of wholes.

8 Continue talking about the process. Are the toothpicks good for keeping the parts on? Are you trying to make it stand up? How can we make it stronger?

9 Respond to the models as they begin to take shape, continue this verbal response until children feel they have successfully completed the art making process. Reflect on the experience. What did children find difficult? Easy? Enjoyable? Extend the experience and try to imagine the models as part of a 'scene'. Where would they live? How can we make a home, an environment for them?

FULFILMENT OF THE EARLY LEARNING GOALS FOR CREATIVE DEVELOPMENT

Goal

- Explore colour, texture, shape, form and space in two and three dimensions.

Fulfilment

- Children explore the properties of clay through the senses.
- Children respond to the Olmec ceramic forms.
- Children explore shape and form of a malleable material.

Goal

- Use their imagination in art and design, music, dance, imaginative and role play and stories.

Fulfilment

- Children explore the uses of clay in other cultures.
- Children imagine life in another time and culture.
- Children think about sequences and steps.
- Children imagine their models as part of a scene. They imagine an environment for their models.
- Children think about the uses for Olmec ceramic models.

Goal

- Respond in a variety of ways to what they see, hear, smell, touch, and feel.
- Express and communicate their ideas, thoughts and feelings by using a widening range of materials, suitable tools, imaginative and role play, movement, designing and making, and a variety of songs and musical instruments.

Fulfilment

- Children will respond to the clay by exploring it through the senses.
- Children respond to Olmec ceramics with their own visual designs.
- Children learn how to use clay as an artistic medium.
- Children begin to see that one media has many uses.
- Children use form and sculpture to communicate ideas.

Background information

There is much information available on Meso-American and Olmec ceramics. Reference materials come from websites, museums, and books. Two websites with fantastic pictures include http://www.humanities-interactive.org/splendors/ex 048_02.html and http://www.bauerart.com/PC_Olmec.html.

Special needs adaptation

Both children with special needs and younger children will need extra support in attaching the pinch pots and in fixing the parts onto the main body of the model.

Colour and art elements 2

COLOUR PAINTINGS

When

Only offer this experience after children have completed Initial painting experience (Experience No. 2) and Colour and art elements 1 (Experience No. 11). This experience can be done using either the 'warm' colours or the 'cool' colours. Our example uses warm colours.

Materials

1 Dripless thick school paint or finger paint (red, orange, yellow).
2 Large white paper.
3 Mixing palette.
4 Assorted brushes.
5 Bowls of water.
6 Photos, reproductions, and any background information (Vincent Van Gogh, Mark Rothko, J.M. Turner; read through experience).

Motivation

1 Bring a variety of different, but solid, coloured materials into the classroom. For example, an orange, a yellow grapefruit or banana, green grapes, a blue scarf, green leaves, purple flowers, a red jumper, etc. Look at each colour, ask children to arrange objects according to colours – what colours look good together, which colours look similar?

2 Children and staff break the objects into groups; separate them into *warm* colours – reds, oranges, and yellows – and *cool* colours – blue, green, and violet. Leave out any white or black objects. Look at all the cool coloured objects; think about how the colours make you feel. Now look at the warm coloured objects – see if you feel any differently.

3 Engage in an aesthetic experience – have children imagine being surrounded by

blue, ask if they would feel warm or cold. Have children imagine being surrounded by orange or red; how would they feel? Introduce children to the idea of warm and cool colours.

4 Now concentrate on one group, in this example we focus on warm colours, and look around the room for colours that are warm.

5 Go outside and look for warm colours – the sun, sand, a red house?

6 Before beginning the art making part of this experience, encounter art by introducing children to some works of art painted in predominantly warm colours (see background information for suggested paintings). How do the paintings make children feel?

Art making

1 Using the works of art as inspiration, encourage children to paint using only warm colours. This does not necessarily mean children create representational paintings. We are only promoting an understanding of colour, not trying to teach realism. Furthermore, though we do not tell children what subject to paint, we need to guide them, offer them some open-ended themes such as 'the outside', 'my pets', 'playing games', or support their suggestions.

2 Children begin to work on large white paper. Support colour mixing and paint application. Note, varieties of warm colours can be made by mixing any combination of red, yellow, and orange.

Possible discussion or dialogue

1 Discuss what colours children like to see together. Ask children why they like certain colours next to each other. Get children thinking about 'colour families'. Make looking at colour an aesthetic experience, enable children to notice variations, how colours make them feel, etc.

2 Ask children what they would feel like if they were surrounded by the colours in the cool group. What about the warm group? Ask, if the colour red was next to you, do you think it would feel hot or cold? Note, many children will say cold, all answers are subjective and of course correct. We are simply teaching proper terminology and encouraging children to see the world in new ways.

3 When looking around both the room and the environment for warm colours, remind children of the names of the warm colours. Think back to the initial lessons on colour and reiterate that there are many different types of one colour. Describe all the oranges, yellows, and reds that you find.

4 Discuss the reproductions of paintings that use mainly warm colours. Ask children what colours the artist used. Encounter art through the senses and ask how many types of yellow, red, orange can you see? How would it feel to be standing in the middle of the painted scene or design? Touch on how colours can stir emotions. Ask 'How does this painting make you feel, happy?' 'Sad?' 'Nervous?' 'Scared?'

5 Before children begin to paint, talk to them about their ideas, use the selected artists' paintings as stimulation for new ideas. Ask, 'What do you imagine when you hear the word warm?'

6 Look at one of the abstract paintings, in this case, artist Mark Rothko (see background information), and encourage children to explore mixing and using warm colours in their visual works.

7 Engage in dialogue during the process. Ask children how they are mixing certain colours, how newly mixed colours are different to colours already on the paper.

8 Respond to the finished creations, how do they make you feel? What kinds of colours did we use? Do they feel warm? Encourage children to talk about the compositions, any frustrations, and their process during the art making experience.

FULFILMENT OF THE EARLY LEARNING GOALS FOR CREATIVE DEVELOPMENT

Goal

- Explore colour, texture, shape, form and space in two and three dimensions.

Fulfilment

- Children explore colour in the environment, in painting, and in three-dimensional objects.
- Children learn about colour by mixing paint.
- Children explore the colours, shapes, and forms of different artists.
- Children explore the implied physical feeling of colour, and touch on the emotions evoked by certain colours.

Goal

- Use their imagination in art and design, music, dance, imaginative and role play and stories.

Fulfilment

- Children imagine being surrounded by a colour.
- Children learn about the imaginative use of colour in the work of various artists.
- Children imagine colour to have a property such as warm or cool.

Goal

- Respond in a variety of ways to what they see, hear, smell, touch, and feel.

- Express and communicate their ideas, thoughts and feelings by using a widening range of materials, suitable tools, imaginative and role play, movement, designing and making, and a variety of songs and musical instruments.

Fulfilment

- Children feel, see, and touch colour.
- Children connect emotions and physical properties to colours.
- Children compare and contrast colour groups.
- Children actively seek out certain colours in the environment.
- Children learn how to use colour to communicate a thought or feeling.
- Children see variety in one colour.
- Children learn how to use colour mixing to communicate or form expression.

Background information

On the colour wheel, cool colours are, generally, green, blue, and violet; warm colours include red, orange, and yellow. Many artists use a colour grouping, such as warm or cool, throughout a composition to communicate emotion, set a mood, or create visual tension. A careful look through an art history reference book or a thorough search on the Internet reveals numerous examples of paintings that employ such methods.

When looking for paintings that use warm or cool colours, ensure your selection is varied, include an abstract work, a semi-abstract work, and, if you choose, a more realistic work. Three good examples of warm paintings useful for this lesson are: Joseph Mallord William Turner, *The Slave Ship* (1840), Museum of Fine Arts, Boston. This painting can be found in many art history books and on the Artchive http://www.artchive.com, click on Turner, then on images.

Vincent Van Gogh, *The Night Café* (1888), Yale University Art Gallery, Connecticut. This image is found in most art history books and on the Artchive, follow the address http://www.artchive.com/, click on Van Gogh and next on the link for 'Arles' (February 1988 – May 1989).

Mark Rothko *Yellowband* (1956), Sheldon Memorial Art Gallery and Sculpture Garden, University of Nebraska-Lincoln. This image, and many like it including *Orange and Yellow* (1956), are available in art history books and on dozens of websites including the Artchive. Follow the address http://www.artchive.com/ and click on Rothko.

The more research the educator does on these artists, the more possibility there is that the discussion about selected artists could lead to new experiences.

Special needs adaptations

Provided children have already explored the other colour and painting experiences, there are no special needs adaptations for this experience.

Printing

POP PRINTING

When

This experience should be encountered after children have completed most exploratory lessons, especially Initial printing experience (Experience No. 3) and any mark making or drawing experiences. Before beginning this lesson educators may wish to remind children of printing methods by engaging children in a shortened version of the Initial printing experience (Experience No. 3).

Materials

1 Water-based printing ink or thick school paint (one colour).
2 Small paint rollers or *brayers* (staff can put the ink on with paintbrushes if rollers are unavailable).
3 White paper (big enough to fit over the Styrofoam printing tray).
4 Pencils.
5 Polystyrene trays (trim the sides to ensure a flat surface to draw on).
6 A flat tray to roll out the ink or paint.
7 Photos, reproductions, and any background information (Andy Warhol; read through experience).

Motivation

1 Remind children of the initial printing experience. Ask children to again make finger or handprints in paint on paper, make at least two of the same finger or handprints on the paper, and set them aside.
2 Bring newspapers (at least two copies of the same one), copies of the same poster or flyer, and a multiple of a book into the classroom. Ask children to look for differences between each of the copies. Look again at the repeated finger or handprints. Encourage children to see a connection between methods.
3 Encounter art and introduce the work of Pop artist Andy Warhol. Show an image of Warhol's that uses multiples (see background information for suggestions).

4 Have an aesthetic experience by looking closely at Warhol's print under a microscope, or greatly enlarge the work; try to find differences in the multiples.

5 Think about how he was able to get the same exact image each time. Did he paint it the same? Trace it? Look again at a copy of a newspaper; think how all of those words could be repeated for so many newspapers.

6 Bring out a painting with only one image (show a painting by any artist or staff can show a single painting by one of the children). Look at the difference between the single image and Warhol's repeated image.

7 Introduce the printing process. Show children the polystyrene trays, rollers, and paints, these materials are incredibly motivating.

8 The magical process of printing will keep the motivation throughout the experience.

Art making

1 Acquaint children with the printing tools; talk to them about making multiples, many of the same picture.

2 Prompt children to draw on the polystyrene with the pencil, make sure they press down hard enough to impress the material. Children can draw some ideas on paper first; educators should have some guiding direction for children regarding subject matter, for example, 'my family', 'faces', or 'the sky'. Alternatively, try doing this project in conjunction with a subject children are particularly interested in at the time, say, for example insects or trains. Remind children of significant and meaningful subject matter.

3 Once children have drawn their image, roll out the ink or paint on a large flat tray, then roll some of the ink over the top of the children's images on polystyrene, make sure there is a thin even coat over the surface of the picture.

4 Demonstrate the steps of taking a piece of paper, placing it on top of the inked image, pressing and smoothing it with the palm of your hand, and finally peeling it away from the polystyrene printing plate.

5 Once you have one image, repeat steps 3 and 4 until each child has reprinted their image at least twice. Note, after a few reprints ink or paint tends to soak into the design on the plate, deeming it unusable.

Possible discussion or dialogue

1 Talk about the initial printing experience. What do children remember? What kinds of prints did they make? Be sure, when children repeat the experience of making a finger or handprint, they are encouraged to talk about the process.

2 Look at and talk about copies of newspapers, posters, or books. Compare the duplicate newspapers with the duplicate finger or handprints children just made. How are they alike? Can we make the same exact print of our finger again?

3 Talk about the work of Pop artist Andy Warhol. Show some of his prints; look closely and ask if each repeated image is the same. Prompt children to look for

differences. Look at colours and shapes within each repeated image. Do the same with two identical newspapers. Ask children how the newspapers are similar to Warhol's prints.

4 Guide children into a dialogue regarding how they think Warhol was able to exactly repeat an image. Ask if he painted it? Traced it? Took a picture of it?

5 Compare Warhol's print with a single painting (choose reproduction of a painting by any artist or staff can show a painting by one of the children). Have children articulate the differences.

6 Engage in dialogue about printing media, ask children to guess what we will do with each of the materials.

7 Talk to children about the printing process, explaining to them the idea of repeating the same image.

8 Talk to children about the imagery they will be using, seek out something significant and meaningful to them, guide their thinking.

9 Support children's dialogue during the process. Do they have to press hard to make an impression into the printing plate? Is the paint or ink easy to roll out? What do they think is going to happen when they lift the paper from the printing plate?

10 Talk about repeating the process. Ask children what they think will happen. Again, refer back to the newspapers and Warhol's prints; encourage children to see the connection.

11 After making a series of prints, lay them out and prompt children to compare each print they made. Relate their multiples to the newspapers and Warhol's work.

12 Respond to the children's work and encourage them to reflect on the process. Encounter art and talk to them about other printed materials (greeting cards, photographic pictures). Discuss ways to use multiple prints as part of another experience or as a useful tool in our daily life. What do we need prints for? How can we use this method in the formation of our own expressions?

13 This is difficult, but try to think back to painting. Ask children if they see the differences between the printing method and painting. Go a step further and compare printing to making clay models or pots – can children articulate the difference? Can they show you the difference?

FULFILMENT OF THE EARLY LEARNING GOALS FOR CREATIVE DEVELOPMENT

Goal

• Explore colour, texture, shape, form and space in two and three dimensions.

Fulfilment

• Children explore and discover colour, shape, space and form through the method of printing.

Goal

- Use their imagination in art and design, music, dance, imaginative and role play and stories.

Fulfilment

- Children think about sequences; how a print was left, an impression made.
- Children begin to understand cause and effect.
- Children imagine how multiples can be used in their own narratives.

Goal

- Respond in a variety of ways to what they see, hear, smell, touch, and feel.
- Express and communicate their ideas, thoughts and feelings by using a widening range of materials, suitable tools, imaginative and role play, movement, designing and making, and a variety of songs and musical instruments.

Fulfilment

- Children respond to the impressions they make on the printing plate.
- Children understand printing as a way to communicate thoughts and expressions.
- Children learn about printing media and methods.
- Children respond to the work of artist Andy Warhol; they investigate his media and methods.
- Children compare and contrast their work with both the work of a famous artist and with meaningful everyday items such as books and newspapers.
- Children begin to think about the differences between media and methods, and between two-dimensional and three-dimensional art.

Background information

In the visual arts, a print is an artwork that is made, not by drawing directly onto the paper, but through a transfer method. Prints, for the most part, tend to be produced in multiples.

A *brayer* is a small rubber roller printers use to roll out and apply ink to the printing plate. Brayers can be found in almost any hobby, craft, or art supply shop.

Andy Warhol (1928–87), an incredibly well-known twentieth-century artist and personality, pioneered the Pop Art movement and became famous by exhibiting and replicating images and objects from popular culture. Information and artworks by Warhol can be found in most twentieth-century art history books and on numerous websites on the Internet (see Appendix 4 for resources). An excellent resource is The Andy Warhol Museum http://www.warhol.org.

Educators should choose Warhol prints in keeping with the 'multiples' idea. Three excellent prints for children to talk about include: *Marilyn Monroe* (1962); *100 Campbells' Soup Cans* (1962); *Twelve Cadillacs* (1962), all Montclair Museum, New Jersey. All of these images can be accessed from the website Artcyclopedia http://artcyclopedia.com; put in a search for Warhol.

Special needs adaptations

There are no special needs adaptations for this experience.

Craft

PAPER MAKING

When

This experience is an initial activity.

Materials

1 Various used paper – any used white or beige paper, coloured sugar paper if colour is desired.
2 A basin with water.
3 Stack of newspaper.
4 Thin natural and man-made materials such as thread, grass, pieces of leaf.
5 A masher.
6 Laundry starch.
7 Natural dyes – dark coloured fruit juice such as cranberry or grape.
8 A small-holed screen larger than A4 size paper.

Motivation

In this experience, as in many, the motivation blends in with the art making process, part of the motivation will be making the paper.

1 Have available varieties of different coloured or textured papers for children to aesthetically experience – touch, see, smell. Think about how paper gets its colour, how texture can be achieved. Think about the different uses for the various papers. Think about where paper comes from.
2 Introduce children to the handmade papermaking process. Begin art making (see next section).
3 When paper is soaking, children should begin to think about how they will decorate their piece of paper. They should think about colour, texture, natural objects.
4 Take children on a walk outside to collect some natural materials, remind

children these objects need to be as 'thin as paper'. Look for stringy grass, flower petals. Back in the classroom press any leaves and grass between books to ensure they adhere to the paper pulp (press for approximately 1 day).

5 Continue with the experience – see the following art making section.

Art making

1 Collect used paper suitable to the lesson. Some excellent examples include notepaper, old white or beige scrap paper, and letters, try to stay away from paper with a finish on it and from newspaper.

2 Children tear the paper into small pieces (approx 3–5 cm). Put torn paper in a tub of water, the tub should be larger than the screen you are using. The ratio of water to paper is approximately two to one, but it will vary depending on how thick you want your paper – staff are encouraged to experiment.

3 Add laundry starch to the water and paper mixture (add approximately two tablespoons of starch for every tub of mixture) and leave the paper to soak for a day or two.

4 After soaking for one to two days, mash any paper that has not disintegrated. Colour can be added as disintegrated sugar paper or from natural materials.

5 Collect paper pulp onto the screen either by dipping the screen directly into the tub and scooping up the pulp or by pouring the paper pulp right onto the screen itself with a ladle or a pitcher. Add until desired thickness. Note, natural materials can be added directly to the pulp before it is poured onto the screen or can be put into the paper pulp when it is on the screen.

6 Hold the screen over the tub, lightly smooth with a sponge, if children have not done so already, ask them to add their materials. Be sure the materials are securely embedded into the mixture.

7 Place a newspaper on top of the pulp and flip entire screen over (the pulp is now face down on newspaper and the screen is on top). Using a sponge, soak up the extra water. Remove the screen, cover with more newspaper, and leave securely pressed under heavy books.

8 Leave paper covered in newspaper for at least 24 hours. After 24 hours, peel away from newspaper and leave to air dry until hard.

Possible discussion or dialogue

1 Have an aesthetic experience. Prompt children to discover the paper samples through their senses. Ask questions that lead them to explore the paper. How does it feel? Is it bumpy, smooth? Does it smell like anything? Look at it under the magnifying glass, under a microscope, what do you see? What is inside the paper?

2 Talk about where paper comes from. Before it gets to the shop, where is it? Seek prior knowledge.

3 Discuss the hand-made papermaking process. Show children all the materials and talk about each one.

4 Discuss the best paper to find and tear up. Talk about using recycled paper, and what recycled means. Discuss coloured paper; what would happen if we added coloured paper? Remind children of natural dyes, if they have already completed the project on tie dyeing (Experience No. 13). Remind children of how we dyed the cloth.

5 Prompt children to talk when they begin the process. Why are they tearing the paper? What happens when it hits the water? What will happen to the paper after it has been in the water for a long time? Will it look the same when we take it out?

6 Discuss the paper as it disintegrates; have an aesthetic experience, engage children in observing the physical changes the paper undergoes.

7 Talk about the materials children wish to add to their paper. Ask if it is possible to add large objects such as acorns, or is it best to add small objects that are thin like paper, such as pressed petals or cotton thread? When children go to gather the materials, listen to their dialogue and guide new knowledge.

8 As the pouring of the paper pulp begins, have a dialogue about the properties of the paper. What is different? How did this happen? What will happen as we pour it through this screen?

9 Ask children to add their gathered materials to their paper. Ask them what they have selected and why. Talk to them about where they are placing the objects. Ask again if an acorn or large object would go in the paper.

10 As you wait for the paper to firm up and dry, talk to children about the experience; ask them what they think the pulp will look like when it hardens.

11 When the paper is dry, reflect on the process and respond to the children's works. Begin to talk about how they can use their paper. What can they use the hand-made paper for? How would they change their paper next time, would they make it thicker? Coloured? Could they make it into a different shape? What about into a form?

FULFILMENT OF THE EARLY LEARNING GOALS FOR CREATIVE DEVELOPMENT

Goal

•   Explore colour, texture, shape, form and space in two and three dimensions.

Fulfilment

•   Children explore the textures, colours, and physical properties of paper.
•   Children think about making form from a two-dimensional media.
•   Children deconstruct and reconstruct a two-dimensional media.
•   Children look at the textures and forms in nature.
•   Children respond to the physical changes of a two-dimensional medium.
•   Children learn how to fabricate colour, texture, and form.

Goal

- Use their imagination in art, design, music, dance, imaginative and role play stories.

Fulfilment

- Children think about where paper comes from.
- Children learn sequencing, and follow the cycle of a process.
- Children imagine the uses for their creations.

Goal

- Respond in a variety of ways to what they see, hear, smell, touch, and feel.
- Express and communicate their ideas, thoughts and feelings by using a widening range of materials, suitable tools, imaginative and role play, movement, designing and making, and a variety of songs and musical instruments.

Fulfilment

- Children think about paper as an artistic medium.
- Children gain control over a medium by exploring, deconstructing, and fabricating it.
- Children discover media through the senses. They investigate paper.
- Children begin to see nature as a provider of artistic media.
- Children discover colour and form through artistic exploration.
- Children use both man-made and natural objects to create both functional and non-functional art.
- Children learn about different paper.

Background information and special needs adaptation

There is no background information or special needs adaptations for this experience.

Construction

ENVIRONMENTAL CONSTRUCTION

When

Use this experience only after children have completed Initial construction experience (Experience No. 4).

Materials

1 Boxes (various sizes).
2 Wooden or Styrofoam blocks.
3 A collection of natural objects (to be found on site).
4 Recycled materials – if set in an urban environment.
5 Paper and pencils.
6 Photos, reproductions, and any background information (Andy Goldsworthy and Christo; read through experience).

In this experience, more than in most, the motivation and the art making are synonymous. Consequently, the two parts are written about under one heading.

Motivation and art making

Begin by asking children to think about the earlier experience in construction. Remind children of what they built, the materials they used, problems they may have run into.

Introduce children to artists who build big constructions in the everyday environment. Educators can use either, or both, Andy Goldsworthy and Christo. Note, Christo would be better for an urban environment, as his constructions are often fabricated with man-made materials. Goldsworthy uses natural materials; learning about his work would suit an environment that has more natural resources available. In time, introduce children to both artists.

In this experience, we focus first on the work of Andy Goldsworthy and, second, on the work of Christo.

For Goldsworthy

1 Encounter art; show children pictures of Goldsworthy's works. Explore his materials; think about the work's significance, what does it mean? Does it have to mean anything?

2 As a group, think about making your own outdoor construction; think about available materials, locations. Note, in this experience educators should guide children to come up with construction ideas that are relevant and meaningful. For example, this experience may take place while children are learning about food, the sea, even letters; link the children's learning in other areas in with this experience. Find a way to make their creation meaningful. For example, if children are learning about food, think about an outdoor construction that involves, possibly, a type of vegetable garden.

3 After discussion, take a walk outside and just look around. Have an aesthetic experience, prompt children to observe the landscape, envision a construction, and scan for natural resources.

4 Back in the classroom, think again about what was seen outside; refer once more to the work of Goldsworthy. If developmentally possible, have children break into groups and design some constructions on paper, in the sand tray, or with wooden blocks.

5 After designing or suggesting some ideas, as a class, choose the most feasible and popular design. Think about how the design will be made, where will it go, and what materials will you need, what size will it be? This part of the project can take a long time, perhaps days. Further, the class will have to go out into the environment on a number of occasions while the designing is taking place.

6 After the project is fully designed, go out into the environment and look around for the natural resources the class has decided it will need to complete the construction.

7 Begin building the construction; the process will certainly cause changes to the original design, model flexibility for the children and adapt to all changes.

8 Be mindful that, as is true with most earthworks and, indeed, many say is the beauty of environmental constructions, they are not permanent. Full photographic and video documentation of both the process and of the final work is essential.

For Christo

1 Encounter art; introduce children to the work of Christo. Think about what Christo builds, what does it mean? Look at his use of materials. Think about how he changes the outside world.

2 As a group think about making your own environmental construction; what kind of materials would you use? Where in the classroom or outside area would you build a construction? Again, just as we looked for relevance and meaning in our designs for outdoor environmental constructions, our indoor constructions, made from recycled and man-made media, must be linked to the children's interest. For

example, children may be learning about a certain country, or they may be interested in dinosaurs. Encourage children to connect this experience with their daily interests. For example, if their interest is in dinosaurs, why not build a dinosaur environment, a place for dinosaurs to sleep?

3 After discussion, take a walk around the classroom or outdoor area, look around and think about some different ideas; look at available resources and spaces.

4 Gather as a group and refer again to the work of Christo. Look at how he used the space; look at his materials. Think about the materials available to us.

5 Educators should have some recycled materials available for inspiration such as boxes, plastic bottles, string, and so forth. Think about how these materials can be used to make something relevant and meaningful.

6 Begin to come up with ideas as a group, and then break into small groups and fashion small models in the sand tray, out of blocks, on paper, or even in clay.

7 After designing some ideas, as a class, choose the most feasible and popular design. Begin to think about actual construction, how the parts will go together, what materials will be used, will it be safe? How long should it be left up for?

8 Begin to gather resources; ask children to look at home, on their way to nursery, visit local resource centres.

9 Begin building the construction; as with most of the experiences, the construction may change and evolve in the process; welcome the evolution.

10 Remember, just as Christo's work is not permanent, neither is ours. The wonderful part of creating this structure is that it is only temporary, and, therefore, very special, novel, and worthy of attention. Full photographic and video documentation of both the process and of the final work is essential.

11 Take the construction down together, document the space when the construction is gone, think about other ways to change the environment.

Possible discussion or dialogue

The dialogue suggestions listed below are divided into two parts, the first for Andy Goldsworthy and the second for Christo; though the dialogue is similar, separating them will makes it easier for educators to implement this experience.

For Andy Goldsworthy

1 Talk to children about their initial construction experience. Remind them of their work, bring out, and talk about past photographs of their fabrications.

2 Introduce the work of artist Andy Goldsworthy. Discuss how he uses nature to create his constructions; how he works with nature, constructs works that 'fit' into the environment, and uses resources he finds right there in the area he is working. Talk about how nature inspires him. Show some pictures of his work. Discuss how they are temporary. Talk to the children about temporary art, ask children what they think happens to Goldsworthy's art in time (see background information for suggested Goldsworthy images).

3 Ask children why they think he makes constructions that will soon be destroyed; relate what he does to their own classroom constructions.

4 Talk about making your own outdoor construction; discuss materials, and available resources.

5 Encourage children to think of meaningful ideas relevant to their needs, likes, or studies in other content areas. Do they want to make a structure for animals to use, an abstract shape in response to the shapes they have been learning about?

6 On your initial exploration outside, just spend time observing. Talk to children about the landscape; mention any hills, patterns, grassy areas. Talk about forms that would fit in with the environment, for example, think about shapes or structures that echo or work in unison with the natural landscape; articulate this to children. Make verbal and written notes about available resources.

7 When coming up with ideas, engage children in a dialogue about their thoughts. Remind them of what they saw outside, talk about Goldsworthy's work, how it fits in with the environment. Discuss work already going on in the class, ask how this project can be made in the context of other ongoing experiences and interests. Talk to all the children about the process they are using to develop their idea – are they making a model? A drawing?

8 Prompt children to describe their ideas to the class. Find links between the ideas, through reflection on their visual designs come up with a collaborative idea.

9 Talk about the basics of the design – what will we need? Is it available? How will we make it? How long will it take?

10 When fabricating the construction, listen out for dialogue that could change the course of the work, enhance the work, exemplify frustrations or difficulties. Ask children if the original plan is still the objective or if unforeseen circumstances, newly found materials, or fresh ideas have changed the course of the project. Have children see the process unfold.

11 When the construction is finished, reflect on the processes used, and respond to the final work. Continue to observe the work in nature. Is it what we wanted? Does it work with the landscape? What is it for? How is it decaying, deconstructing, breaking up over time? What can we add to this structure? What else does the landscape need?

For Christo

1 After reminding children of their previous constructions, introduce children to the work of Christo. Look at pictures of his work; ask children what materials he uses. Do we find those materials in nature? Do they belong in nature? Talk about where he fabricates them. How do they look in the environment? Would you see his work everywhere? Have you ever seen anything like it? How does he change the outside? Do you think he keeps the work up forever? (See background information for suggested Christo images.)

2 Ask children why they think he makes constructions that will soon be dismantled; relate what he does to their own constructions. Talk to children about how his work is not in a museum, but right outside in the environment.

3 Talk to children about making their own construction. What materials are available? Engage in a discussion about recycled materials. The educator should show children some examples of these materials such as boxes, lids of jars, and the like – the list is endless. Ensure anything provided is safe and hygienic.

4 Before coming up with any ideas, discuss the spaces such a construction might fit into. On your initial walk around the chosen areas, note the size, shape, and other physical properties of the area.

5 Talk with children as they begin to come up with ideas. Encourage children to think of meaningful ideas relevant to their needs, likes, and studies in other content areas. Remind children the structure does not have to 'be' something. Look again at Christo's works; remind the children that their construction can be there just to look at, as a design. Continue to remind children of available materials. Talk to all the children about the process they are using to develop their idea – are they making a model? A drawing?

6 Prompt children to describe their ideas to the class. Find links between all the children's ideas; through reflection on their visual designs come up with a collaborative idea.

7 Talk about the basics of the design – what will we need? Are the materials available? Easily accessed? Who will get them and how? How will we make it? How long will it take? How long should the construction be up for? Who will see it?

8 When fabricating the construction, listen out for dialogue that could change the course of the work, enhance the work, or exemplify frustrations or difficulties. Ask children about the media they are using, are they experiencing any difficulties? Is this what they thought the construction would look like? Remind the children of their processes.

9 When the construction is finished, reflect on the processes used, and respond to the final work. Observe the work in the environment. Does the piece work in the space? Does it fit in or does it look as though it does not belong there? Did our materials suit the purpose? Is it what we hoped for? More? Less? If the work is in an outside area or in a corridor, along with the children, watch how people respond to the work. Do they stare at it? Smile? Encourage children to talk about how they themselves feel about the work.

10 When dismantling the work, listen for dialogue about extended activities, use of materials, or further transformation of the educational environment. Talk to children about the process of taking the construction apart, how is it different to building it? Does it feel different? Is it quicker? Why? Discuss how the space feels without the construction. Does it feel emptier now than before we built the work? Continue discussing the transformation of space, look for links to another experience.

FULFILMENT OF THE EARLY LEARNING GOALS FOR CREATIVE DEVELOPMENT

The fulfilment of the early learning goals for both artists is discussed in this experience.

Goal

- Explore colour, texture, shape, form and space in two and three dimensions.

Fulfilment

- Children look at a space, and explore the idea of form in space.
- Children explore the textures, shapes, colours, and forms of natural or recycled materials when choosing media for fabricating a construction.
- Children think about how much space is used by forms.
- Children create a three-dimensional form.
- Children respond to the forms made by other artists.
- Children look at the uses of some two-dimensional objects in the creation of their three-dimensional forms.

Goal

- Use their imagination in art and design, music, dance, imaginative and role play and stories.

Fulfilment

- Children think about sequences.
- Children use their imagination to think about what will happen next.
- Children track their process.
- Children use their creations in stories or role plays; the creations become backdrops, or part of the scenery.

Goal

- Respond in a variety of ways to what they see, hear, smell, touch, and feel.
- Express and communicate their ideas, thoughts and feelings by using a widening range of materials, suitable tools, imaginative and role play, movement, designing and making, and a variety of songs and musical instruments.

Fulfilment

- Children begin to see construction as a way to communicate ideas and give form to expression.
- Children employ the proper media for construction, and learn what will and will not fit, work, or be suitable to their intended construction.
- Children expand their knowledge about materials that can be used to shape their thoughts or ideas.
- Children respond to suitable colours, textures, shapes and forms by using them in their constructions.
- Children gain inspiration from nature, art history, everyday objects.
- Children see nature as a provider of materials and as a place to create visual expression.
- Children understand space as a potential tool in their constructions.

Background information

Artist Andy Goldsworthy (b. 1956) is celebrated for his incredible environmental constructions that use materials and resources found on site. Goldsworthy fabricates art that works in unison with the natural landscape. Staff can find information and images in a number of books by the artist himself, and websites.

Suggested imagery includes: *pebbles with hole* and *broken pebbles*. Both images can be found on the website for the Center for Global Environmental Education http://www.cgee.hamline.edu/, run a search for Goldsworthy and follow the link Andy Goldsworthy. Other Goldsworthy images can be found on http://www. sculpture.org.uk.

Sculptor Christo (b. 1935) is a pioneer of Land Art; his creations use the natural or constructed environment as a backdrop or canvas. He aims to merge or marry art with the chosen environment. There is much information available on the artist; images from his constructions are plentiful, as are videos and sketches of the process involved in the making of the works. It is suggested that educators use one of Christo's most famous works entitled *Running Fence*, Sonoma and Marin Counties Coast, 1972–76 and *Wall of Oil Barrels, Iron Curtain*, 1961–62, Rue Visconti, Paris. Both of these images can be accessed on the website Christo and Jeanne-Claude http://www.christojeanneclaude.net/ Jeanne-Claude is Christo's wife with whom he collaborates. To view both of the suggested works, click on the link for Christo and Jeanne-Claude's photo collection. *Running Fence* is located under that link; for *Wall of Oil Barrels, Iron Curtain* click on a second link titled 'earlier works'.

Special needs adaptation

This experience does not require any adaptations for children with special needs; however, as this experience can be physically challenging, educators should offer support to those children at a younger physical developmental level.

Mixed media and craft

EXPLORING QUILTING

When

Use this experience after children have explored collage, mark making, shapes, colours, and have had some experience with textiles.

Materials

The materials for this experience will depend on the children's needs and the skills of the educator. Listed below are a selection of materials staff and children may need for any number of ends.

1 Sugar paper (approximately 25 × 30 cm), for quilting sections.
2 Assorted sugar paper for collage.
3 Glue sticks.
4 White card (approximately 25 × 30 cm).
5 Child's scissors.
6 Yarn.
7 Hole punch.
8 Felt tips.
9 Pencils.
10 Extra white paper for sketches.
11 Photos, reproductions, and any background information (quilting books; read through experience).

Motivation

1 Encounter art; introduce children to quilts and quilting. Think about the uses of quilts. Show children different quilts used for different purposes. Ensure quilts are shown from a variety of cultures. See background information for resources.
2 Read to the children one of the books about quilting included in the background information section.

3 After looking at pictures of quilts and, if possible, real quilts, encourage children to think about making their own quilt. Make the quilt relevant and meaning-ful, relate it to another experience or a topic the children have been exploring; consider the various types of quilts – commemorative, narrative, family and community symbolism. Think how the children's needs and interests can link in with a certain type of quilt. For example, perhaps the quilt will tell a story about the children, or maybe it will serve to commemorate an occasion of relevance to the children.

4 When children have decided upon a theme, educators should prompt children to think about their individual part of the quilt.

5 Show the children the media they will be using; remind children of collage techniques, shapes, lines. Show children the difference between the media we will use and the media of a fabric quilt.

6 Have children work on some initial sketches for their quilt section.

Art making

1 After a thorough exploration of the theme, support children in the creation of their individual quilt section.

2 Give each child one white card section. Children will then use mixed media, including the crayons, felt tips, and collage method to create their composition. Note, because of vast differences in developmental levels, some of the children's work will be highly symbolic, while others will be more of an exploration of media. All types of visual outpourings will work together in the final quilt.

3 When children have finished their section, lay them all out on the floor. In between each of the children's sections, place a section of coloured sugar paper. With the help of children start to put all of the sections into a pattern, in the overall shape of a large rectangle (see Figure Ex. 20.1). Educators will have to count how many sections will be needed to form a rectangle. If extra sections are needed, think about adding another plain section of coloured sugar paper.

4 Prompt children to come up with a way of putting the sections together to give a feeling of unity, balance, harmony.

5 When the right composition and combination of sections have been selected, punch holes in the touching edges of each section (punch the holes where you would normally sew the sections together).

6 With the help of children, use the yarn through the punched holes and begin to stitch the sections together.

Possible discussion or dialogue

1 Discuss with children the art of quilt making. Begin by talking about blankets, textiles, fabrics. Introduce pictures of quilts; it would make a tremendous impact on the children's understanding if a real quilt could be exhibited.

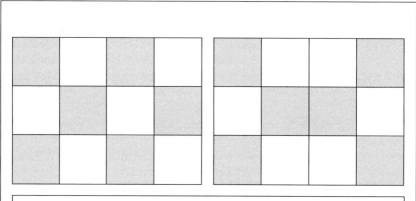

Form quilting patterns by placing coloured sugar paper in between sections of children's work. Collaborate with the children when creating the final quilt composition. In this illustration, the patterned squares represent the sugar paper.

Figure Ex. 20.1 Quilting patterns

2 Talk about the sections of the quilt, the patterns, about what quilts represent, how they serve a multitude of purposes. Discuss how they are sometimes used to keep us warm and other times only meant to be looked at like a painting.

3 After a book on quilting is read, take some time to engage in dialogue about the story.

4 Discuss with children the idea of making their own quilt out of paper. Remind children that the quilts we have been learning about are made with fabric.

5 Get children engaged in a dialogue about how quilts can symbolise an event. Tell a story, or how some quilts are made only in celebration of patterns, colours, designs.

6 Talk to children about themes relevant in their life. Did something happen recently they would like to commemorate in a quilt? Alternatively, have they been discovering colours and shapes and would simply like to make a quilt to further explore these new concepts? At this time, also talk about where the quilt will go. Look at and discuss different spaces with children; relate the purpose of the quilt to the space where it will hang.

7 Talk to children about their individual quilt section; encourage them to talk out their ideas as they sketch them.

8 Discuss the idea of mixed media with the children. Support dialogue that talks about the combination of the mediums. During the process, ask children how the collage looks on top of the crayon, or how the felt tips look over collage.

9 When all the sections are finished, start laying them out on the floor, creating a patterned effect using coloured sugar paper between the children's sections. Talk

to the children while you set the sections down. Model for children looking at pattern, trying to make the composition harmonious; ask children to help you do this. Ask children where they think certain sections should go and why.

10 As a group, talk about the almost finished composition, does it look like it goes together? Is there anything we should move around? Look at and talk about any pattern created.

11 Discuss sewing with the children, compare it with the Exploring weaving and craft (Experience No. 8). Ask children what is similar between the two processes. Different?

12 When the quilt is completed and hung up in the chosen area, prompt children to reflect on the process and respond to the final work. Is the quilt unified? Does it 'go together'? Does it communicate our theme, purpose? If children have completed construction (Experience No. 19), ask how this experience relates. Working together? Creating something for the environment? Link the quilt making experience with other collaborative works that sometimes tell a story, symbolise a community, or are created to beautify the environment such as murals; begin to think about possibilities in mural painting.

FULFILMENT OF THE EARLY LEARNING GOALS FOR CREATIVE DEVELOPMENT

Goal

• Explore colour, texture, shape, form and space in two and three dimensions.

Fulfilment

• Children explore shape, colour, form and space by looking at and responding to quilts, working with art media, and creating their own paper quilt.

Goal

• Recognise and explore how sounds can be changed, sing simple songs from memory, recognise repeated sounds and sound patterns and match movements to music.

Fulfilment

• Children discover visual patterns and repeated shapes.

Goal

• Use their imagination in art and design, music, dance, imaginative and role play and stories.

Fulfilment

- Children think about narratives and sequences.
- Children use their imagination to envision the final quilt.
- Children use their imagination in coming up with the design for their section of the quilt.
- Children work together, coming up with imaginative solutions and ideas.
- Children listen to a story about quilting.

Goal

- Respond in a variety of ways to what they see, hear, smell, touch, and feel.
- Express and communicate their ideas, thoughts and feelings by using a widening range of materials, suitable tools, imaginative and role play, movement, designing and making, and a variety of songs and musical instruments.

Fulfilment

- Children create their own quilt in response to learning about the art of quilt making.
- Children learn that quilts can be used to express stories, themes, ideas, and thoughts.
- Children learn how mediums can work together. How one type of medium may be more suitable in expression than another medium.
- Children learn how art can be used to commemorate an occasion.
- Children learn about collaboration, and how collaboration is used in art making.
- Children explore the concept of functional and non-functional art.

Background information

Images and information on quilts and quilting can be found in craft, art, and reference books, and in abundance on the Internet. Some websites include The World Wide Quilting Page http://www.ttsw.com/mainquiltingpage.html; About.com http://www.quilting.about.com; and Quilting with Children http://www.thecraftstudio.com. Museums are another valuable resource for quilting images and information, museums that feature quilting include the Textile Museum of Canada, http://www.museumfortextiles.on.ca; the New England Quilt Museum, http://www.nequiltmuseum.org; and the American Folk Art Museum http://www.folkartmuseum.org.

Books to read to children include: Jeff Brumbeau, Gail De Marcken (Illustrator) *The Quiltmaker's Gift*, Pfeifer-Hamilton (2001); and Ann Jonas, *The Quilt*, Puffin, (1994).

Special needs adaptation

Special needs children may need to use adapted scissors.

Extended and further experiences

DRAWING

Extended experiences in:

- Learning lines – straight, curvy, zigzag, up, down, spiral, thin, thick, short, long.
- Learning shapes – circle, square, triangle, rectangle, oval.
- Learning forms – round, flat, heavy, light.
- Learning marks – smudge, dot, flick, thick, thin.

New experiences with drawing media, tools, and techniques:

- Using natural and man-made media.
- Drawing with sticks, grass, pencils, charcoal.
- Surfaces to draw on (bumpy, smooth, coloured, paper, bark, rocks).
- Resist techniques (wax, glue, string).
- Rhythm and movement, mixed media, combining shapes and lines, patterns, responding to works by artists.

PAINTING

Extended experiences in:

- Colour mixing, colour theory, expressive colours.

New experiences with painting media, techniques, and tools:

- Explore brush techniques (splatter, stroke, tap).
- Surfaces to paint on (canvas, paper, wax paper, tissue, bark, fabric).
- Textures to paint on (bumpy, smooth, lined, indented).
- Watercolours, sand painting, sugar painting, sponging, marbling, glue painting, mixed media, resist techniques, natural and man-made paints.

PRINTMAKING

Extended experiences in:

- Mono printing, stamping, rolling, rubbing, impressing.
- Printing with natural and man-made objects.
- Looking at patterns and markings.

New experiences with printing media, tools, and techniques:

- Explore textures, rhythm, and pattern.
- Learn about the printing press.
- Print with two colours.
- Woodcut, linoleum prints, plaster and sand prints, rubber-stamping, sponge, glue, string, cut paper, rag, eraser prints, and vegetable prints.
- Printing on a selection of surfaces (cling film, wax paper, canvas, card).
- Printing for various reasons (cards, wrapping paper).
- Explore artists' prints, the difference between printing and painting.

CERAMICS

Extended experiences in:

- Rolling, pounding, pulling, modelling, pinching, manipulating clay, and creating textures.
- Caring for clay, learning about objects made from clay, and the properties of clay.

New experiences with clay media, tools, and techniques:

- Learn coil technique, subtractive modelling (carving the form out of clay), slab method.
- Firing methods (pit, kiln).
- Make a clay house, village, or person.
- Finishing techniques (painting, glazing, varnishing).
- Pottery wheel, functional and decorative art, studio pottery, ceramic sculpture, explore ancient cultures.
- Compare old ceramic methods with modern techniques.

TEXTILES

Extended experiences in:

- Texture (rough, smooth, bumpy, thin, thick, spongy).
- Visual properties (patterned, shiny, see-through, webbed, coloured, sparkles).
- Dyeing (man-made dyes, natural dyes, creating patterns).
- Weaving, quilting.
- Textiles for role-play, costumes, collage.
- Caring for fabrics, learning about objects made from textiles.

New experiences with textiles:

- Clothing design, costume history.
- Learning about threads, yarns, ropes, natural textiles and man-made fabrics.
- Crayon transfers, batik, decorating fabric, beading, furniture covering.
- Functional and decorative textiles, textiles for survival.
- Carpets and rugs, knotting, sewing, knitting, looms, tapestries, fabric quilting.

COLLAGE

Extended experiences in:

- Tearing, paper and fabric textures, cutting, gluing, making shapes.
- Using nature in collage.

New experiences with collage:

- Natural collages, recycled collages, three-dimensional collage, tissue paper collage, mural collages, collage books, magazine or newspaper collages.
- Mixed media (painting, drawing, printing with collage).
- Mosaic; explore artists who use collage.

CONSTRUCTION

Extended experiences in:

- Building, collecting, using natural, recycled, and man-made materials, adhering and connecting parts.
- Exploring the constructed environment.
- Creating functional and decorative constructions.

New experiences with construction media, tools, and techniques:

- Creating paper constructions (folding, cutting, gluing, connecting paper products).
- Decorating surfaces of constructions (painting models, blocks, natural objects).
- Using different wood, scraps, and materials, building with papier-mâché, newspaper and tape.
- Creating the frames and skeletons for models.
- Constructing puppets, scenery for role play or puppetry, building environments.
- Translating two-dimensional work into three-dimensions.

Art materials

When it comes to art materials, staff need to be resourceful; few educational settings have unlimited funds for the arts. Seek donations, collect from nature, or call museums and galleries and ask for images. Staff can try visiting a paper or other mill and see what treasures they are getting rid of, or check if the town or city has a local play resource centre (with a good search, readers will find these resource centres are all over the country, offering educators, sometimes free, but usually just very inexpensive materials). Below is a non-exhaustive list of basic art materials; recognise art experiences do not depend on a huge investment in expensive art materials, they depend on staff dedication, insight into the importance of art, and the implementation of the methods and approaches presented in this book. There are many settings with plenty of art materials, but without knowledge of appropriate art practice, materials are worthless; materials alone cannot teach art. Finally, remember, provided materials are safe, there really are no rights or wrongs when it comes to media. With creative thinking, the list of materials children can use in artistic experiences is endless.

DRAWING TOOLS

Thick and thin wax crayons, washable thick and thin felt tips, oil pastels, coloured and white chalk, soft pencils, thick and thin vine charcoal, coloured pencils, non-toxic fixative, drawing boards, sketchbooks (some cartridge paper stapled or clipped to heavy paper or cardboard makes a wonderful makeshift sketchpad).

PAINTING MEDIA

Finger paint in small pots; finger paint is not only for painting with fingers, it is wonderful for young children, it does not drip and it is very easy to handle. Many of the lessons in this book use finger paint instead of tempera paint. Tempera paint, powder paint, watercolour paint, water containers.

BRUSHES

Flat, round, very thick, and very thin brushes, and brushes with long and short handles. Brushes are used for paint, water, and glue in a multitude of projects; staff may want to think about designating certain brushes for particular media, for example, set aside some brushes to be used with glue only.

PAPER

Various shaped paper – long, square, rectangular, oval, circular. Paper of various weights, colours, textures. Tissue, tracing, newsprint, wax paper, and aluminium foil. Paper for tearing, constructing, drawing, painting, and printing on. Paper for sketches, doodles, and important scribbles.

PRINTING MEDIA

Water-based printing ink, soft-rubber brayers, small paint rollers, trays, stamps, sponges, plastic table covers, and a selection of printing surfaces.

CERAMICS

Air-dry and natural clay (store in sealed containers), wooden clay tools (tongue depressors, wooden spoons, and the like), rolling pins, sponges, wooden boards with canvas stretched over them (good for rolling clay out onto), small pots for water and clay waste, buckets with lids for storage.

CONSTRUCTION

Wooden blocks, sand, wire, scrap wood, cardboard, and tools for cutting and adhering.

TEXTILES

Various fabrics (textured, coloured, patterned, plain, selection of sizes), yarn, thread, fabric crayons, cardboard looms, stapler, masking tape, dyes (man-made and natural).

NATURAL MEDIA

A vast selection of natural objects including a collection of shells, sticks, twigs, leaves, stones and rocks, materials to draw and make marks with, create texture with, print with, sculpt with, build with, draw, paint, and print on. Natural media to observe, draw, and discover, products to extract colour from.

OTHER MATERIALS

Children's scissors, string, palettes, masking tape, glue (PVA), glue sticks, glue spreaders, felt, recycled and found objects, bulldog clips, touchy feely boxes, texture wall, shadow boxes, bubbles, microscopes, kaleidoscopes, magnifying glasses, mirrors.

UNSAFE ART MEDIA

Permanent felt tips, toxic fixative, ready-made papier-mâché (pre-mixed wallpaper paste), epoxy glues, sharp points and blades (including corners and sides of card and paper), non-water based paints.

Art reference

Listed is a brief reference for use in encounters with art. To put the art of every culture, artist, or art movement into a perfect timeline is beyond the scope of this Appendix. This being the case, what is offered here is simply geographical regions educators may want to reference, or the general features of the art of cultures, countries, periods, or artistic movements. For detailed information, staff should consult art appreciation and history reference materials.

PRE-HISTORIC ART (EUROPE)

Palaeolithic Period 35000 BC – 8000 BC, Mesolithic Period 8000 BC – 3900 BC, Neolithic Period 4000 BC – 1500 BC: cave art: Lascaux, Dordogne region, France, rock paintings, megaliths: Stonehenge.

ART OF THE ANCIENT NEAR EAST

Mesopotamia (today Iraq and Syria), Iran, Eastern Mediterranean (Israel, Lebanon, Jordan), Arabian Peninsula, Anatolia (Turkey).

ART OF EGYPT

Early Dynastic Period, Old Kingdom, Middle Kingdom, New Kingdom, Late Period: Stepped pyramid at Saggara, Pyramids of Giza, rock-cut tombs, Beni Hasan, Temple of Amen-Re, Karnak, Tomb of Tutankhamen.

ART OF GREECE

Art of the Aegean: Cycladic and Minoan: pottery (large storage pots), architecture, small figurative sculpture, Geometric period, Archaic period: pottery design, vase painting, sculpture, Classical period: architecture, sculpture, the Acropolis: the Parthenon, Temple of Athena Nike, Hellenistic period: relief sculpture, sculpture, architecture.

ROMAN ART

Etruscan, Roman republic, Imperial periods: tombs, mosaic, sculpture, portrait sculpture, relief sculpture, architecture: Pompeii, Colosseum, the Pantheon.

ISLAMIC ART

Architecture, textiles, pottery, functional and decorative art, books, tiles: mosques of Spain, India, Jordan.

ART OF INDIA

Architecture, textiles, sculpture, fresco, painting: the Great Stupa, Buddha image, temples, cave painting, Hindu cave temples, Vishnu temple, rock-cut temples.

ART OF CHINA

Shang Dynasty, Chou Dynasty, Ch'in and Han, T'ang, Sung, Yuan, Ming, and later dynasties: ceramic soldier statues in Tomb of Emperor Shih Huang Ti, bronze, relief sculpture, Buddha images, ink and colours on silk (scrolls), ink on paper, landscape painting, porcelain.

ART OF JAPAN

Pottery, architecture, textiles, scrolls, painting, printmaking, tea ceremony: gardens, landscape painting, realism, Kabuki theatre, Katsura Palace.

ART OF MESO-AMERICA (CENTRAL AND SOUTHERN MEXICO, NORTH CENTRAL AMERICA)

Olmec: stone sculpture (large and small-scale), relief sculptures, West Mexico / pre-Columbian: clay sculpture, effigy figures, Maya: architecture, temples, relief sculpture, sculpture, Teotihuacán and Aztec: temples, sculpture.

ART OF SOUTH AMERICA (ANDEAN CULTURES)

Chavin, Peruvian art (Mochica culture, Tiahuanaco, Inca): stone sculpture, ceramics, temples, spouted vessels, portrait bottles, textiles, Inca architecture.

INUIT ART

Ornamentation, masks, beads, carving, leatherwork.

NATIVE AMERICAN ART

Plains (examples, Sioux, Pawnee, Cheyenne): beadwork, carved pipes, decorated clothing and quillwork, drawing.

Southwest – Pueblo, Apache, Navajo, Pima, Pueblo (various groups including Hopi and Zuni): architecture, pottery, Kachina dolls, murals from kivas, silverwork inlaid with stones. Navajo, Apache, and Pima: basketry, weaving, silverwork, sand paintings.

The Plateau, Great Basin, and California – dozens of groups include, for example, Nez Perce and Ute: basketry, cornhusk bags, and beadwork.

The Southeast (for example, Seminole, Cherokee, Creek): Mound Culture, beadwork pottery, basketry, jewellery with shells, ornamentation, stone carvings.

Northeast Woodlands (for example, Iroquois, Algonquian): pottery, beadwork, metalwork, masks, quillwork, woodwork.

Northwest Coast (for example, Tlingit, Haida): carving, totem poles, beadwork, canoes, long houses, blanket weaving, masks.

AFRICAN ART

Art produced in all parts of the massive continent. Woodwork, masks, rock painting, ceremonial objects, pottery, bronze, sculpture, textiles, small figures, relief sculpture, stools, body ornamentation.

OCEANIC ART

Australia, Polynesia, Micronesia, New Guinea: carving, monoliths, body ornamentation, woodwork, masks, spirit figures, canoes.

BYZANTINE ART

Mosaics, architecture, painting, sculpture.

MEDIEVAL, ROMANESQUE, GOTHIC ART

Painting and illumination, books, metal objects, architecture, sculpture, stained glass.

EARLY RENAISSANCE, THE RENAISSANCE

Paintings with tempera on wood, fresco, architecture, sculpture, painting, relief sculpture: the Vatican, Sistine Chapel, Leonardo Da Vinci, Michelangelo, Titian, Albrecht Dürer, Raphael.

BAROQUE ART

Painting, fresco, sculpture, architecture, portraits: Caravaggio, D. Velazquez, P. Rubens, Rembrandt, J. Vermeer, Christopher Wren.

ROCOCO, ROMANTICISM, NEOCLASSICISM, REALISM

Painting, architecture, furniture, sculpture, landscapes, political painting: Watteau, F. Boucher, T. Gainsborough, Sir J. Reynolds, B. West, J.L. David, F. Goya, E. Delacroix, T. Géricault, J.A.D. Ingres, J.M.W. Turner, J. Constable, T. Cole, J.F. Millet, H. Daumier, E. Manet, J.S. Sargent, R. Bonheur, G. Courbet, W. Homer.

IMPRESSIONISM, POST-IMPRESSIONISM, EXPRESSIONISM, REALISM

Painting, sculpture, mixture of art styles and movements: C. Monet, A. Renoir, E. Degas, C. Pissarro, G. Seurat, P. Cézanne, Van Gogh, P. Gauguin, Toulouse-Lautrec, E. Munch, A. Rodin, C. Claudel, W. Homer, H. Rousseau.

TWENTIETH-CENTURY ART MOVEMENTS AND ARTISTS

Twentieth-century art is very difficult to categorise into neat units of artists and their movements. This being the case, rather than attempting to pigeonhole artists into certain movements or styles, two separate lists are offered. The first is a selection of art movements, groups, or styles, and the second is a general listing of modern artists whose work many children find appealing. Note, the list of artists is very limited; readers will find many artists not included on the list, others have already been mentioned with a grouping in the previous section. If artists of major influence have been left out all together, apologies in advance. It is indeed impossible to list each artist children and staff will find exciting.

Always consult an art history book before embarking on an experience that involves a particular artist or style.

MODERN ART MOVEMENTS OR GROUPS

Fauves
Blue Rider group
Expressionism
Art Nouveau
Cubism
Futurism
Dada
Surrealism
Abstract Expressionism

Abstract Formalism
Action painting
Social Realism
Op Art
Land Art
Pop Art
Conceptual Art
Constructivism
Fluxus

Hyperrealism
Kinetic Art
Installation Art
Computer-generated art
Harlem Renaissance
Staged Photography
Multi-media art

TWENTIETH- AND TWENTY-FIRST-CENTURY MODERN ARTISTS

Albers, J.
Arp, J.
Basquiat, J.M.
Bearden, R.
Beuys, J.
Bourgeoise, L.
Calder, A.
Chagall, M.
Chamberlain, J.
Christo
Close, C.
Dali, S.

De Chirico, G.
De Kooning, W.
Derain, A.
Dine, J.
Douglas, A.
Dubuffet, J.
Duchamp, M.
Ernst, M.
Escobar, M.
Estes, R.
Flack, A.
Flavin, D.

Freud, L.
Gaudi, A.
Giacometti, A.
Goldsworthy, A.
Gorky, A.
Gris, J.
Hanson, D.
Haring, K.
Hepworth, B.
Hesse, E.
Hirst, D.
Hockney, D.

Hodgkin, H.
Hoffman, H.
Hopper, E.
Johns, J.
Judd, D.
Kahlo, F.
Kapoor, A.
Kelly, E.
Klee, P.
Klimt, G.
Kline, F.
Lawrence, J.

Leger, F.

Lichtenstein, R.

Magritte, R.

Marc, F.

Marin, J.

Miro, J.

Modigliani, A.

Mondrian, P.

Moore, H.

Motherwell, R.

Nevelson, L.

Newman, B.

Noguchi, I.

O'Keeffe, G.

Oldenburg, C.

Orozco, J.

Paik, N.J.

Pearlstein, P.

Pfaff, J.

Picasso, P.

Pollock, J.

Rauschenberg, R.

Ray, M.

Reinhardt, A.

Richter, G.

Riley, B.

Rivera, D.

Rothenberg, S.

Rothko, M.

Segal, G.

Serra, R.

Shahn, B.

Shapiro, M.

Skoglund, S.

Smith, D.

Smithson, R.

Stella, F.

Still, C.

Tapies, A.

Tinguely, J.

Twombly, C.

Vasarely, V.

Warhol, A.

Whiteread, R.

Wood, G.

Wright, F.L.

Wyeth, A.

Museum and gallery information

The following selection of resources aims to support visual art teaching in the early years. Museums, books, and resources listed reflect this specific subject.

MAJOR MUSEUMS AND GALLERIES

The British Museum
Great Russell Street
London WC1B 3DG
Tel. 020 7323 8000
http://www.thebritishmuseum.ac.uk

The Design Museum
28 Shad Thames
London SE1 2YD
Tel. 020 7940 8790
http://www.designmuseum.org

Hayward Gallery
Belvedere Road
London SE1 8XX
Tel. 020 7921 0600
http://www.hayward.org.uk

Livesey Museum for Children
682 Old Kent Road
London SE15 1JF
Tel. 020 7639 5604
http://www.liveseymuseum.org.uk

Museum of Childhood at Bethnal Green
Cambridge Heath Road
London E2 9PA
Tel. 020 8980 2415
http://www.museumofchildhood.org.uk

National Gallery
Trafalgar Square
London WC2N 5DN
Tel. 020 7747 2885
http://www.nationalgallery.org.uk

Natural History Museum
Cromwell Road
London SW7 5BD
Tel. 020 7942 5011
http://www.nhm.ac.uk

National Museum and Gallery Cardiff
Cathays Park
Cardiff CF10 3NP
Tel. 029 2039 7951
http://www.nmgw.ac.uk/nmgc

National Museum of Photography, Film and Television
Bradford
West Yorkshire BD1 1NQ
Tel. 01274 202030
http://www.nmpft.org.uk

National Portrait Gallery
St. Martin's Place
London WC2H OHE
Tel. 020 7306 0055
http://www.npg.org.uk

Pitt Rivers Museum (world archaeology)
South Parks Road
Oxford OX1 3PP
Tel. 01865 270927
http://www.prm.ox.ac.uk

Royal Academy of Art
Burlington House
Piccadilly
London W1J OBD
Tel. 020 7300 8000
http://www.royalacademy.org.uk

Tate Gallery
Millbank
London SW1P 4RG
Tel. 020 7887 8000
http://www.tate.org.uk/britain

Tate Liverpool
Albert Dock
Liverpool L3 4BB
Tel. 0151 702 7400
http://www.tate.org.uk/liverpool

Tate Modern
Bankside
London SE1 9TG
Tel. 020 7887 8000
http://www.tate.org.uk/modern

Tate St Ives
Porthmeor Beach
St Ives
Cornwall TR26 1TG
Tel. 01736 796226
http://www.tate.org.uk/stives

Victoria and Albert Museum (decorative and applied arts)
Cromwell Road
South Kensington
London SW7 2RL
Tel. 0870 442 0808
http://www.vam.ac.uk

Whitechapel Art Gallery
80-82 Whitechapel High Street
London E1 7QX
020 7522 7878
http://www.whitechapel.org

Visit the Art Museum Network http://www.amn.org for information, images, exhibitions, and news from museums around the world.

Selected books, websites and other useful information

A trip to the library or a search on the Internet for art history will uncover more information than any educator could possibly need. Offered here is a small selection of some classic (and user-friendly) art history books and websites.

REFERENCE BOOKS FOR EDUCATORS

Art Through the Ages: Renaissance and Modern Art, H. Gardner, R.G. Tansey, F. Kleiner (eds) Harcourt Brace College Publishers, US (1995).
History of Art, H.W. Hanson and A.F. Hanson, Thames and Hudson (2001).
The Art Book: Mini Edition, A. Butler, Phaidon Press (1997).
The Story of Art, E.H. Gombrich, Phaidon Press (1995).

BOOKS FOR CHILDREN

Brown Bear, Brown Bear What Do You See? Bill Martin, Eric Carle (Illustrator), Puffin Books (1995).
Camille and the Sunflowers, Laurence Anholt (Illustrator), Frances Lincoln, (1995).
Degas and the Little Dancer, Laurence Anholt (Illustrator), Edward Degas (Illustrator), Frances Lincoln (1999).
Gregory and the Magic Line, Dawn Piggot, Orion Children's (2002).
I Am an Artist, Pat Lowery Collins, Robin Brickman (Illustrator), Econo-Clad Books, (1994).
Katie Meets the Impressionists, James Mayhew, Orchard (1998).
Katie's Picture Show, James Mayhew, Orchard (1993).
Kipper's Book of Colours, Mick Inkpen (Illustrator), Hodder Children's Books. (1997).
Let's Go to the Art Museum, Virginia K. Levy, Abrams (1988).
Maisy's Book of Colours, Lucy Cousins (Illustrator), Walker Books (1999).
My Many Colored Days, Dr. Seuss, Steve Johnson (Illustrator) Lou Fancher (Illustrator), Alfred A. Knopf (1996).

Picasso and the Girl with the Ponytail, Laurence Anholt (Illustrator), Frances Lincoln (1998).
A Potter, Douglas Florian, Greenwillow (1991).
Touch and Feel: Shapes, Dorling Kindersley (2000).
A Walk in Monet's Garden, Francesca Crespi (Illustrator), Frances Lincoln (1995).

WEBSITES

General images

World Art Treasures – http://www.bergerfoundation.ch
WebMuseum! – http://www.sunsite.unc.edu/wm
Artchive – http://www.artchive.com
Artcyclopedia – http://www.artcyclopedia.com
Art Museum Image Consortium – http://www.amico.org
Tate Collections – http://www.tate.org.uk/collections

Also, visit the websites of museums listed in this Appendix for needed images and reproductions.

Specialist

Ancient World Web – http://julen.net/ancient
Artserve – http://rubens.anu.edu.au (art from Mediterranean Basin and Japan)
ChristusRex – http://www.christusrex.org (Vatican images)
African Art – http://www.uiowa.edu/~africart
National Museum of American Art – http://nmaa-ryder.si.edu
Asian Arts – http://www.webart.com/asianart/index.html
Kyoto National Museum – http://www.kyohaku.go.jp
Islamic Art – http://www.Iacma.org/Islamic_art/thumbnails/thmbnail.htm
Art Timeline from the Metropolitan Museum of Art http://www.metmuseum.org/toah/splash.htm

Professional organisations

International Society for Education Through Art (InSEA)
Cito/InSEA
P.O. Box 1109
NL 6801BC Arnhem
The Netherlands
Fax: +31 26 3521202

National Society for Education in Art and Design (NSEAD)
The Gatehouse
Corsham Court
Wiltshire SN13 OBZ
England
Tel. 01249 714825

International Child Art Foundation (ICAF)
1350 Connecticut Ave NW
Washington, DC 20036–1702
United States
Tel. + (001) 202 530 1000

Funding

Arts Council of England
14 Great Peter Street
London SW1P 3NQ
Tel. 020 7973 6590
http://www.artscouncil.org.uk

Contact the Arts Council of England for regional arts board contact details, information on the arts, funding, lottery and grant programmes, training, and news.

Artist in residence

The following offer excellent guidance for educators wishing to bring an artist into their classroom or school.

- *Artists in Schools*, Caroline Sharp and Karen Dust, National Foundation for Educational Research (NFER) (1999).
- *Artists in Residence*, Sally J. Manser and Hannah Wilmot, London Arts Board and St. Katherine and Shadwell Trust (1995).
- *Art Professionals in Schools – a step by step guide to artists in schools projects*, Keith Winser, Norfolk Educational Press.
- Cardiff Arts in Education Agency (caea)
  Southey Street
  Roath
  Cardiff CF24 3SP
  Tel. 029 2049 3425
  http://www.caea.org.uk

References

Anderson, F.E. (1994) *Art-Centered Education and Therapy for Children with Disabilities*. Springfield, IL: Charles C. Thomas.

Arnheim, R. (1969) *Visual Thinking*. Berkeley, CA: University of California Press.

Arnheim, R. (1983) 'Perceiving, thinking, forming', *Art Education*, 36 (2): 9–11.

Baker, D. (1992) *Toward a Sensible Education: Inquiring into the Role of the Visual Arts in Early Childhood Education*. (Report No. PS 021 325). Urbana, IL: Conference on Making Meaning Through Art (ERIC Document Reproduction Service No. ED 356 080).

Barnes, R. (1987) *Teaching Art to Young Children 4–9*. London: Routledge.

Brittain, W.L. (1979) *Creativity, Art, and the Young Child*. New York: Macmillan Publishing Co., Inc.

Bruner, J.S. (1961) *The Process of Education*. Cambridge, MA: Harvard University Press.

Chapman, L. (1978) *Approaches to Art in Education*. New York: Harcourt Brace Jovanovich, Inc.

Colbert, C.B. (1995) 'Developmentally appropriate practice in early art education', in C.M. Thompson (ed.) *The Visual Arts and Early Childhood* (Report No. SO025112). Reston, VA: National Art Education Association (ERIC Document Reproduction Service No. ED383643).

Cole, E. and Schaefer, C. (1990) 'Can young children be art critics?' *Young Children*, 45(2): 33–43.

D'Amico, V. and Buchman, A. (1972) *Assemblage*. New York: The Museum of Modern Art.

Delacruz, E.M. (1995) 'Multiculturalism and the tender years: big and little questions,' in C.M. Thompson (ed.) *The Visual Arts and Early Childhood* (Report No. SO025112). Reston, VA: National Art Education Association (ERIC Document Reproduction Service No. ED383643).

Department for Education and Skills (DFES) (2002) 'Special educational needs in England: January 2002 provisional,' statistics from the Annual Schools' Census 2002. Online. Available HTTP: http://www.dfes.gov.uk/statistics/DB/SFR/s0332/index.html (accessed 3 November 2002).

Drummond, M.J., Rouse, D.R. and Pugh, G. (1992) *Making Assessment Work*. Nottingham Group and National Children's Bureau.

Edwards, L.C. and Nabors, M.L. (1993) 'The creative art process: what it is and what it is not,' *Young Children*, 48(3): 77–81.

Eglinton, K.A. (2002) 'Sharing good practice: intervention in art,' *Nursery World*, 102(3834): 22–23.

Eisner, E.W. (1972) *Educating Artistic Vision*. New York: Macmillan.

Eisner, E.W. (ed.) (1976) *The Arts, Human Development, and Education*. Berkeley, CA: McCutchan Publishing Corporation.

Eisner, E.W. (1985) 'Why art in education and why art education,' in *Beyond Creating: The Place for Art in America's Schools*. Los Angeles: The Getty Center for Education in the Arts, pp. 64–69.

Eisner, E.W. (1988) 'On discipline-based art education: a conversation with Elliot Eisner' (interview with Ron Brandt), *Educational Leadership*, 45(4): 6–9.

Eisner, E.W. and Ecker, D. (1966) 'What is art education?' In E. Eisner and D. Ecker (eds) *Readings in Art Education*, Waltham, MA: Blaisdell, pp. 1–27.

Feeney, S. and Moravcik, E. (1987) 'A thing of beauty: aesthetic development in young children,' *Young Children*, 42(6): 7–15.

Gardner, H. (1976) 'Unfolding or teaching: on the optimal training of artistic skills,' in E.W. Eisner (ed.) *The Arts, Human Development, and Education*. Berkeley, CA: McCutchan Publishing Corporation, pp. 99–110.

Gardner, H. (1980) *Artful Scribbles: The Significance of Children's Drawings*. London: Jill Norman, Ltd.

Gardner, H. (1988) 'On assessment in the arts: a conversation with Howard Gardner' (interview with Ron Brandt). *Educational Leadership*, 45(4): 30–34.

Gardner, H. (1989) 'Zero-based art education: an introduction to ARTS PROPEL,' *Studies in Art Education*, 30(2): 71–83.

Gardner, H. (1990) *Art Education and Human Development*. Los Angeles: The Getty Center for Education in the Arts.

Gaspar, K. (1995) 'Liberating art experiences for preschoolers and their teachers,' in C.M. Thompson (ed.) *The Visual Arts and Early Childhood* (Report No. SO025112). Reston, VA: National Art Education Association (ERIC Document Reproduction Service No. ED383643).

The Getty Center for Education in the Arts (Getty) (1985) *Beyond Creating: The Place for Art in America's Schools*. Los Angeles: The Getty Center for Education in the Arts.

Gilliatt, M.T. (1983) 'Art appreciation: a guide for the classroom teacher,' *Educational Horizons*, (61)2: 79–82.

Hagaman, S. (1990) *Aesthetics in Art Education: A Look Towards implementation*. Bloomington, IN: Adjunct Clearinghouse for Art Education at the ERIC Clearinghouse for Social Studies Social Science Education (ERIC Digest EDO-SO-90–11).

Henley, D.R. (1992) *Exceptional Children Exceptional Art*. Worcester, MA: Davis Publications, Inc.

Herberholz, B. and Hanson, L. (1995) *Early Childhood Art*. 5th edn, Dubuque, IA: Brown and Benchmark. (Original edition 1974).

Honigman, J.J. and Bhavnagri, N.A. (1998) 'Painting with scissors: art education beyond production,' *Childhood Education*, 74(4): 205–211.

Kantor, R. and Whaley, K.L. (1998) 'Existing frameworks and new ideas from our Reggio Emilia experience: learning at a lab school with 2- to 4-year-old children,' in C. Edwards, L. Gandini and G. Forman (eds) *The Hundred Languages of Children*. 2nd edn, Greenwich, CT: Ablex Publishing Corporation, pp. 313–333.

Katz, L.G. (1994) *The Project Approach*. Champaign, IL: University of Illinois at Urbana-Champaign (ERIC Document Reproduction Service No. EDO-PS-94–6).

Online. Available HTTP http://ericps.crc.uiuc.edu/eece/pubs/digests/1994/lk-pro94. html (accessed 28 October 2002).

Katz, L.G. (1998) 'What can we learn from Reggio Emilia?' in C. Edwards, L. Gandini and G. Forman (eds) *The Hundred Languages of Children*. 2nd edn, Greenwich, CT: Ablex Publishing Corporation, pp. 27–45.

Keiler, M.L. (1977) *The Art in Teaching Art*. 2nd edn, Lincoln, NE: University of Nebraska Press (original edition, 1961).

Kellogg, R. (1969) *Analyzing Children's Art*. Palo Alto, CA: National Press Books.

Kerlavage, M.S. (1995) 'A bunch of naked ladies and a tiger: children's responses to adult works of art,' in C.M. Thompson (ed.) *The Visual Arts and Early Childhood* (Report No. SO025112). Reston, VA: National Art Education Association (ERIC Document Reproduction Service No. ED383643).

Kindler, A.M. (1995) 'Significance of adult input in early childhood artistic development,' in C.M. Thompson (ed.) *The Visual Arts and Early Childhood* (Report No. SO025112). Reston, VA: National Art Education Association (ERIC Document Reproduction Service No. ED383643).

Kindler, A.M. (1996) 'Myths, habits, research, and policy: the four pillars of early child-hood art education,' *Arts Education Policy Review*, 97(4): 24–30. Online. Available HTTP: http://www.aea11.k12.ia.us/curriculum/earlych.html (accessed 21 October 2002).

Kolbe, U. (1993) 'Co-player and co-artist: new roles for the adult in children's visual arts experiences,' *Early Child Development and Care*, 90: 73–82.

Leeds, J.A. (1989) 'The history of attitudes towards children's art,' *Studies in Art Education*, 30(2): 93–103.

Logan, F. (1955) *Growth of Art in American Schools*. New York: Harper and Brothers. Online. Available HTTP: http://www.noteaccess.com/APPROACHES/ArtEd/History/ Logan/1940s.htm (accessed 21 March 2002).

Lowenfeld, V. and Brittain, L. (1987) *Creative and Mental Growth*. 8th edn, New York: Macmillan (original edition, 1964).

Papalia, D.E. and Olds, S.W. (1993) *A Child's World*. 6th edn, New York: McGraw-Hill Inc. (original edition, 1975).

Qualifications and Curriculum Authority (QCA) (2000) *Curriculum Guidance for the Foundation Stage*. London: QCA.

Rinaldi, C. (1998) 'Projected curriculum constructed through documentation – *Progettazione*,' in C. Edwards, L. Gandini and G. Forman (eds) *The Hundred Languages of Children*. 2nd edn, Greenwich, CT: Ablex Publishing Corporation, pp. 113–125.

Ring, K. 'Young children drawing: the significance of the context', paper presented at the British Educational Research Association Annual Conference, Leeds, September 2001. Online. Available HTTP http://brs.leeds.ac.uk/~beiwww/beid.html (accessed 8 June 2002).

Schaefer, C. and Cole, E. (1990) *The Museum and Me: An Early Childhood Education Model*. (Report No. PS020469). OH: The Toledo Museum of Art Early Childhood Program (ERIC Document Reproduction Service No. ED 343721).

Schiller, M. (1995) 'An emergent art curriculum that fosters understanding,' *Young Children*, 50(3): 33–38.

Seefeldt, C. (1995) 'Art – a serious work,' *Young Children*, 50(3): 39–45.

Syzba, C.M. (1999) 'Why do some teachers resist offering appropriate, open-ended art activities for young children?' *Young Children*, 54(1): 16–20.

Thompson, C. and Bales, S. (1991) '"Michael doesn't like my dinosaurs": conversations in a preschool art class,' *Studies in Art Education*, 33(1): 43–55.

Wright, S.K. (1994) 'Assessment in the arts: is it appropriate in the early childhood years?' *Studies in Art Education*, 36(1): 28–43.

Index

O(